Get Help!

The Complete Guide to Household Help

by Susan Zolla and Pepper Abrams

Harmony Books/New York

Published by Harmony Books, a division of Crown Publishers, Inc., One Park Avenue, New York, New York 10016 and simultaneously in Canada by General Publishing Company Limited.

HARMONY and colophon are trademarks of Crown Publishers, Inc.

Manufactured in the United States of America

This book was previously published privately in 1983 by A to Z Publishing Company

Illustrator: Janet Salter

Cover: Julie Skoller

Library of Congress Cataloging in Publication Data

Zolla, Susan, 1946–
Get Help!

Bibliography: p.
Includes index.
1. Domestics. I. Abrams, Pepper. II. Title.
III. Title: Household help.
TX331.Z64 1984 640'.46 84-554

ISBN 0-517-55341-4

10 9 8 7 6 5 4 3 2 1

First Harmony Edition

To my husband Ed, whose love and support are invaluable,
and to Alissa, Mimi, and Anne.

Susan Zolla

To Bud, David, Jonathan, Matthew, Susan, and Benjamin —
my treasures.

Pepper Abrams

ACKNOWLEDGMENTS

Many people helped to make this book possible. They contributed ideas, facts, considerations, corrections, and technical information. We recognize and appreciate the editorial and organizational skills of Betsy McIlwain and Vicky Pasternack. We received many ideas from Vicki Faerstein, Jean Root, Laurie Holz, Tomasina Gonzales, Merle Culver, Rose Selesnick, Betty Zolla, Diane Rosenthal, Ana Serrano, Lynne Cohen, Dell Arthur, Barbara McLoughlin, and Karen Bruck.

We thank the many fine people from Harmony Books who supported this book and believed in it. We especially thank Roslyn Siegel and Bruce Harris.

Miguel Ramirez, Victoria Shemaria and Terry Scharf contributed professional advice. Nothing could appear in print without the typing, word processing, and proofreading skills of Sandy Raymer, Betsy Pollock and Claire Sullivan.

We thank the following for sharing their experiences as employers, as employees, or as both: Lois Reinis, Cliff Williamson, Nancy Goldman, Toby Salter, Brenda Adams, Linda Lowitz, Laura Young, Joan Abrams, Jane Doctor, Susan Livingston, Lynne Hiller, Hetwig Swensen, Marilyn Kornhandler, Jan Wilson, Andi Harrow, Barbara Lawrence, Carol Gordon, Nancy Levy, Fred Diaz, Amanda Carmel, David Carmel, Patti Friedman, Francine Goldstein, Leslie Parness, Harriet Glazier, Francie Okun, Mimi DeBlasio and Rosalinda Delgado. Thank you to all others who completed survey forms. Translations into English were made by Gloria Garcia.

Lay-out and design ideas were contributed by Aramaki Design, Faye Elkins, and Tom McIlwain.

Finally, we fully acknowledge that there would be no book without the perspective, knowledge, and support given to us by Alicia Paca, Esperanza Galicia, Leticia Sandoval, and Elba Martinez - thank you.

CONTENTS

INTRODUCTION 11

CHAPTER ONE.................................. 13

INTRODUCING HOUSEHOLDS WITH HELP — INCLUDING OUR OWN

Susan • Pepper • Single But Not Helpless • The Single Parent • Beneficial Partnership for Household Worker • A Two Career Family •Housekeeping as a Career • Successful Homemaker • Housekeeping as a Temporary Job

CHAPTER TWO.............................. 27

DECIDING TO GET HELP

"But Won't I Feel Guilty Having Someone Else Do My Housework or Childcare?" • "But Aren't Servants Only for the Wealthy?" • "Who Are Household Workers?" • "But I Don't Have Room for a Live-In" • "But I Need My Privacy" • "But I Don't Speak a Foreign Language" • "But Will My Children be Able to Communicate?" • "But I Am Worried About My Ability to Act as a Boss" • "But Aren't Most Non-English Speaking Housekeepers Illegal Aliens?" • "But Aren't Housekeepers One More Group of Exploited Workers?" • "I Never Feel Exploited"

CHAPTER THREE.......................... 37

"WHAT KIND OF HELP DO I NEED?" THE AVAILABLE ALTERNATIVES DEFINED

General Job Classification • Daily Cleaning Person • Cleaning Crew • Laundry Help • Cook • Driver • Seamstress • Companion for Elderly or Handicapped • Companion in a Convalescent Home • Shopper/Errand Person • Babysitter, Au Pair, Governess • Nanny • Live-In or Live-Out Housekeeper • Houseman • Hiring More Than One Employee • Temporary Help — A New Baby, A Convalescent Patient, Moving, House for Sale, Entertaining, Houseguests, Out-of-Town.

CHAPTER FOUR........................... 47

"WHAT DOES HOUSEHOLD HELP COST?"

Wages for Live-Out Employees, Day Cleaners, Drivers, Etc. • Wages, Hours, and Working Conditions for Live-In Workers • Minimum Wages • Meals and Lodging • What Does This Really Mean? • The Current Wage Rate for Live-In Employees • "What Else Determines Wages?" • Paid and Unpaid Days Off • Extra Pay • Payroll Keeping • Payroll Cost — Employment Taxes • Income Reporting for Undocumented Foreign Employees • Raises • Pay Period • "Money Isn't Everything"

CHAPTER FIVE........................... 61

HOW TO AFFORD HOUSEHOLD HELP

Add Up What You Are Spending Now • Affording Part Time Help • Careful Spending • Tax Credits for Childcare or Dependent Care • Alternative Ways to Afford Help • Subtle Financial Considerations

CHAPTER SIX........................... 71

INTERVIEWING AND HIRING

"How Do I Find Someone?" • Why Word of Mouth • Placing Ads • "What About Calling an Agency?" • Describe the Job • How to Interview • What to Ask • What to Look for • What to Ask References • Assessing the Information • Not Sure?

CHAPTER SEVEN........................... 83

WORKING AND LIVING CONDITIONS

How to Start the First Day of Employment • Accouterments Provided — Bedroom for Live-In Employee • Meals • "Where Does an Employee Eat?" • "Am I Responsible for Their Dinner When We Go Out?" • Transportation • "What About Uniforms?" • "Health Checks?" • "Gifts?" • Telephone — Employee Personal Use • Answering Your Phone • Visiting With Friends on the Job • Suggestions for Socializing • Night School • Night Socializing • Automobile Use • Keys • That "Evening In Paris" Perfume Driving You Crazy?

CHAPTER EIGHT 95

PREPARING FOR HOUSEHOLD HELP

Putting Your Own Home in Order • "What Cleaning Supplies Should I Provide?" • Professional Supplies • Prepare a Schedule • Sample Daily Schedule for Once a Week Cleaning • Monthly, Biannual, or Yearly Cleaning Jobs

CHAPTER NINE 103

TRAINING HOUSEHOLD HELP

"How Do I Begin Training an Inexperienced Person?" • Laundry Training • Food Storage • Grocery Shopping • Training to Cook • Meal Service • Driving • Training a Non-Driver to Drive • Training a Companion for the Elderly or the Handicapped • If You Are Never Home • Hire a Consultant

CHAPTER TEN 119

INTRODUCING A CHILDCARE PERSON TO YOUR HOUSEHOLD

"Who's She, Mommy?" • What is Your Role? • The Role of Your Childcare Person • Role of Your Child • Where Everything is Kept • Working Together

CHAPTER ELEVEN 125

TRAINING A CHILDCARE PERSON

Babies • Additional Duties With All Children • Suggested Activities for Your Child and Your Housekeeper, Play, Kitchen Crafts, Games, and Quasi-Learning Activities for Non-English Speakers • Activities Not Allowed • Keep This in Mind: If You Want a Playground Director, Hire One • Childcare Training Classes

CHAPTER TWELVE............................133

THE MOST COMMON CHILDCARE ISSUES
AND WHAT TO DO ABOUT THEM

Jealousy • Improper Feeding • Discipline • Remaining the "Real Parent" • When the Housekeeper Leaves Your Job • To Make a Housekeeper's Leaving Easier on Your Child • Leaving the Children With the Housekeeper When You Go Away • "Can I Take the Housekeeper With Us on Vacation?" • "What Do I Do if I Suspect Child Abuse?"

CHAPTER THIRTEEN..........................147

PROMOTING GOOD WORK PERFORMANCE

Ten Steps Toward Effective Home Management • Promoting Good Work Performance With an Employee Whose Good Work is Questionable • Managing Two or More Workers • Ineffective Management Styles: The Tyrant, The Guilty Manager, The Giver, The Missionary, The Hinter, Wisher, and Story Teller, The Dormat, The "I Don't Care Manager" • Be You • How Two Employers See Their Management Role

CHAPTER FOURTEEN.........................157

IRONING OUT THE WRINKLES

The Bottom Line • Breaking or Damaging Personal Property • Stealing • Avoid Scapegoating • Employee Personal Problems — Financial, Health, Pregnancy, Consumer • Extent of Employer Involvement

CHAPTER FIFTEEN............................165

PARTING OF THE WAYS

"Can I Expect to Be Successful With My First Household Employee?" • "When Do I Fire Someone Immediately?" • "How Do I Fire Someone on the Spot?" • Inappropriate Employee Conduct • "How Do I Know Whether My Problems With One Particular Person are Serious Enough to Terminate Employment?" • "How Do I Terminate Employment?" • How to Handle Letting Someone Go Whom You Have Liked • What are the Reasons That Employees Resign • What to Do When an Employee Gives Notice • Empty Closet — When an Employee Leaves Without Notice • Bigotry — For Losers Only • Successful Relationships

APPENDIX

Section 1. EMERGENCY INFORMATION — Getting Emergency Assistance • Telephone List • Prevention of Home Accidents • First Aid

Section 2. IMMIGRATION INFORMATION — What to Tell Undocumented Employees • Expired Visas • Undocumented Workers • The Bureau of Immigration and Naturalization • Applying for Legal Residency • Becoming a Citizen

INTRODUCTION

"Behind every successful woman I know with a public as well as a private life, there is another woman. The dirty little secret is all successful women have household help," wrote Gail Sheehy, in a series of articles about successful women for *The New York Times,* January 17, 1980.

The woman who learns to pay for household help, the woman who learns to delegate authority, may indeed have a greater chance of becoming successful than her counterpart who, resentfully or halfheartedly performs all housework herself. Regardless of whether we choose to be a successful career person, a successful spouse or parent, or a combination of the above, the struggle for all of us is to achieve some degree of self-fulfillment performing whatever role or combination of roles we have chosen.

Throughout history, housework has remained both a necessity and a responsibility assigned to women. Even the most recent research has shown that married career women perform the majority of the household tasks. Husbands do not share equally in the household responsibilities. Perhaps life would seem more fair if men assumed a more equitable share of the work at home. But they do not. Nor has the machine and computer age freed women from ironing shirts or from pushing the vacuum. Hiring household help does free men and women from some of the time consuming tasks that must be done in any household. When a couple pays someone else to wash the dishes, the question of whose-turn-it-is tonight becomes a non-issue. Affordable household help can benefit all involved.

The concept of hiring help may take time to embrace and accept because paid household help is fraught with myth, misunderstanding, and lack of knowledge. Many people lack any personal experience with paid help. For some, hired help is still associated with slavery; for others, hired help is associated with luxury, not with practical, successful home management. *Get Help* will dispel the myths, clarify the misunderstandings and add much practical knowledge to a previously unexplored subject.

The purpose of the book is to legitimize household employment and to give the employer/employee relationship strength and validity. There is no need for the subject of household help to remain dirty, little, or secret. One of our grandmothers was paid to clean homes. We feel no shame. Housework is a legitimate job. If performing it all yourself is no longer pleasurable or practical, read *Get Help*!. If your current employee is not helpful, *Get Help!* will teach you how to be an effective employer.

CHAPTER ONE

Introducing Households with Help—Including Our Own

Susan:

Some people credit their happiness to their discovery of an energizing, rejuvenating power source. The hundreds of joggers who sweat past my home every morning swear that jogging has brought new meaning to their lives. Others credit meditation, a career change, aerobic dancing, or some other force for lifting them out of the muddle and inspiring an awakened belief in themselves. I swear by household help.

The employment of someone to wash the dishes, clean my home, iron my clothes, and watch my children has allowed me to become who I want. I can jog, change careers, do aerobic dancing or any activity I choose because I have given myself the gift of time.

My husband does well and we can afford help. But that was not always the case. I employed cleaning help even when many others with our income would have found this an unaffordable luxury. In the early days when Ed worked as a labor consultant and I as a junior high teacher, we employed a cleaning crew to clean our tiny house every week. We called them "Euphoria and the Refrigerator Cleaners". "Euphoria" — because that is what I felt when I came home after she had been there — and the "Refrigerator Cleaners" because the two men who cleaned also ate everything in the refrigerator.

The birth of our first baby, Alissa, changed our life-style, even though for her first six months I fought this change. At first, I resolved that having a child would in no way impair my ability to remain a school administrator. So, finding a day care home for our baby, I went back to work when Alissa was six weeks old. Day care wasn't my first choice but I was certain that I would get used to it. I did not. Each night I would come home from work, walk to the day care home and be handed a tired and hungry baby, a bundle of dirty clothes and bottles, a list of complaints about her behavior and a big pang of guilt.

Working and day care no longer made sense. Why should I be developing education programs for others when I was not becoming involved in the development of my own child? I resigned from my job and stayed home. But I was not at all prepared for the feeling of helplessness, loneliness and depression that came with staying home. The loss of income was unsettling, but even more distressing was the loss of personal identity and public contact. I was unhappy and angry. I didn't want to work full-time any more but I didn't want to feel trapped and depressed by staying home full-time either. What did I want? I wanted more flexibility in planning each day. I wanted to find part time work projects outside of the home such as buying and remodeling houses. What I needed was control over when I could leave the house and some control over what I could accomplish when I was home.

Finally the realization struck me. The only way to have more control over my own time would be to hire full-time, live-in help. I didn't care who it was or what it cost. It seemed clear to me that my mental health was at stake. One week of full-time help was going to cost less than one hour in psychotherapy.

I called an employment agency and asked for the least expensive live-in candidate. I hired Hilma after a two minute interview. She had just told me that she was not interested in doing much housework but wanted to attend night school and learn English. Since she spoke no English yet and I spoke no Spanish, I assumed that she had told me in Spanish that she loved to iron. At her feet was a rolled up grocery store bag containing all her worldly possessions. She needed to begin living-in at once. I undid my dining room, bought and installed a portable metal closet, and hung an extra towel in the bathroom. I began a new life.

I had been a reasonably effective manager when I worked for the school district or as a contractor. Yet the mistakes I made as an employer could fill a book. Actually, you are holding it.

She was underpaid and given little job benefits. She received no training and no instruction, but she got plenty of hints on how to improve her cleaning. Although she was very good with Alissa, I felt her time with my baby was a threat to my competence as a mother. Ed did not do much better as an employer. He viewed Hilma's presence as a sign of his increased social status and expected her to demonstrate servile and constant attention to his needs. He felt that Hilma would totally relieve me of all household responsibility. Additionally, he felt that since he had paid Hilma to do jobs that were once his, I should be eternally grateful. Not surprisingly, Hilma left without notice two days before the birth of our second baby, Mimi. Ed and I learned from our experiences with Hilma, and our experience has shaped future work relationships.

I have employed a variety of home workers since Hilma. Each one has contributed to my well being and to the well being of our home and family. We have all gained a home environment that supports us and that allows us to go forward.

My employment of household help has also connected me with many lifestyles, age groups, and cultures that my family and I may not have ever been able to experience.

Relationships form. But no work relationship in this house has ever been totally trouble-free. The woman I now employ, Alicia Paca, and I have a relationship that is flexible enough to allow disagreements. Her presence and her work give me the ability to choose a direction for myself, to devote good time to my children, (Annie brought the number to three girls), my husband, any work project and myself. Household help is my energy source; it is my support group.

Pepper:

> *"Yes, it's true. I do have two live-in housekeepers...but it wasn't always that way. My husband, Buddy, and I were married in 1969 and for five debt-free, child-free, care-free years we enjoyed our jobs (as an attorney and teacher, repectively) and had little concern for household matters. Meals were take out and housecleaning was minimal.*
>
> *But life changes. Out first son, David, was born in 1974 and 14 months later came Jonathan. It didn't occur to me to hire a live-in housekeeper just to help me when I was home. But when I wanted to be involved outside the home by teaching three days a week, I hired a day worker named Gloria to care for my sons. My days were filled and fulfilling, but exhausting, and I was very demanding on Buddy. I wanted to hand him a baby for each arm as he walked through the front door and then hide in the bathroom until the children were asleep, but Buddy claimed that's not the way it was supposed to be. He said that unless I hired a live-in within seven days, he was moving out. Since it was cheaper to hire live-in help than support two residences, our convertible den was converted and a housekeeper moved in. I converted quickly, myself, to appreciating the benefits of live-in help.*

We had two healthy children, good jobs, a beautiful home and a loving housekeeper. But life is full of surprises that are not always fair. In that year our son, David, was diagnosed with leukemia and our happy home disintegrated overnight. His first hospitalization was for eight days. I was with him morning and night. Angela, our housekeeper, took over with Jonny as Buddy spent his time in a daze between home and the hospital. For at least the next six months I was unable to function in any capacity. Angela's presence was invaluable. She took care of all of us.

David is almost nine years old now. He has severe emotional problems, extreme learning disorders and continues to suffer from drug side effects. He requires, however, almost continual adult care, and needs help with normal everyday tasks like getting dressed. But he's here with us. Leukemia takes the lives of more children than any other disease yet fifty percent of those diagnosed survive. David appears to be one of the "lucky" ones.

I got pregnant and had Matthew within a year of David's diagnosis. Having an additional child was security for me; and I didn't want Johathan ever to be an only child. This sentiment has proven very ironic because following Matthew came Susan and then Benjamin, all within three years. That added up to five children under the age of six.

By the time we had all five children, we were under the constant stress of hospital visits and new babies. The maintenance of our large family required full time help. The most practical solution seemed to be to hire a second live-in person so, that's what we did.

We currently employ two housekeepers whose work days overlap and whose skills complement each other. Esperanza Galicia is like the children's second grandmother and sometimes mine. She does a lot of the child care and all of the laundry. Our second employee, Lette Sandoval, drives, markets and cooks.

Over the years, many people have worked in our home under a variety of job descriptions and job conditions, but each has worked successfully because they each know that their work is valued. Bud and I need to be able to give our children lots of attention and still provide for David's special needs. Having two housekeepers allows Buddy and me to spend pleasurable time with our children in a variety of activities. All five are developing into people we are proud of.

Household help has also allowed Buddy and me to devote a good deal of time to the Ronald McDonald House, a facility near Children's Hospital of Los Angeles which houses children and their families while children receive medical treatment. I have had the time to create something positive out of David's illness. I began and currently operate a non-profit summer camp for children with cancer. "Camp Good Times" has brought much happiness to so many families that I have found my role extremely rewarding. Such an accomplishment would have been impossible without the assistance of household help."

Single But Not Helpless

Both men and women can operate more efficiently with paid help

Margaret Schaffer is a 32 year old single woman who up until two years ago had never thought of hiring household help of any kind. She currently owns and operates two office equipment stores and employs a day cleaning person to clean once a week.

"After six years of working my way up in the computer business, I wanted out of corporate management and a chance to be on my own. I was preparing to leave my job and open a retail store. The planning

sessions were long and exhausting. I still did all my own housework because I enjoyed it, but I had let everything go for really almost a month. One day I realized that I had a crucial bank meeting the next afternoon and I had neglected to wash my clothes for over three weeks. I quickly went home, gathered everything and took them to the first laundry that promised to have everything clean by the next morning. The next day I dashed over to the laundry right before my meeting with the loan officers. The laundry had lost my clothes, all of them. Oh, I went on to my meeting but I think I got the loan because I looked so pitiful.

That night I felt frustrated and stupid as I sat in my very dirty house with stripped beds, no towels and empty underwear drawers. I telephoned a former roommate and asked her if she knew anyone who could come and clean for me. She gave me the telephone number of a woman named Helen. I called and Helen has worked for me for the last two years. She cleans the stores on Sunday and Monday, cleans my house on Tuesday, does the wash on Wednesday, and cleans my boyfriend's apartment on Thursday.

I don't need to be unorganized. My stores cannot operate unless they are orderly and neither can I. I don't mean sterile and spotless. I mean that everything is where it belongs and everything is ready to function. Helen does a fine job. The beginning of our relationship was a little different for me. But I caught on. She is a valued assistant as much as anyone else and receives the same benefits and a high hourly wage.

My mother cannot believe that I actually pay someone to clean my house and wash my clothes. But then she has trouble understanding that I own my own business and that I have not gotten married..."

The Single Parent

The single parent, male or female, can benefit from paid household help.

T.J. Ross is 34 years old. She is a self supporting, single mother who has managed some degree of success by employing various types of household help. She had live-in help when her 12 year old son was younger and now employs a young woman who comes to her house every day at 3 and leaves between 7 and 9 p.m. five days a week.

> *"I am a working mother. I work for money, not fulfillment, so I have to show up at my job every day. Household help for me is a necessity.*
>
> *I used to keep looking for Mary Poppins, but let me tell you, she does not exist. Or maybe I could never afford her. There have been several good women who have taken care of Jonah over the years and some not so good. Having a housekeeper was still a better childcare alternative for me than some sort of day care outside of my home. It is really less expensive, allows my son to play in his own neighborhood and to be able to stay home when he is sick. A housekeeper gives me total freedom from housework and also the opportunity to date. Household help has really provided my home with a second adult.*
>
> *I have Leslie now, who is not a live-in housekeeper but who drives Jonah and who is paid to wash the dishes, make dinner and do more than just babysit. I always hire whoever is available at the moment I need someone. I don't have much interview time available. Sometimes my hiring method is to hold up the mirror and if the breath of life appears, I hire.*
>
> *I got married at age 19 and had Jonah when I was 22. I hired my first housekeeper because I had to. Really, I knew nothing about the responsibilities of motherhood. My own mother couldn't be much help,*

so she sent me $500 and told me to call an agency and hire someone. Mitchell, my husband, didn't object, so I called an agency and they sent me Linda. She was an angel of mercy, expecially with the baby.

When my son was ten months old, Mitchell took off with another woman. It was a terrible time for me, full of grief and frustration. Having household help meant that I could go to my room, cry for a week, and not see anyone. Linda took care of the baby and helped me through that very dark and angry time.

After Mitchell left, I got a full-time job. It was financially tough to pay Linda's salary. As a matter of fact, I could just about pay the rent out of my salary. Yet Linda took a pay cut and even bought cleaning supplies herself because she knew I was stretching my budget to keep her. We formed a partnership to try to help each other out, financially and emotionally.

I guess I originally hired a housekeeper because I didn't know what I was doing. I was unprepared for motherhood. I thought a baby could die if I did something wrong. After I went to work full time, I employed housekeepers because I needed someone to care for my son. For me now, hired help is a way of life."

Beneficial Partnership for Household Worker

Today, Linda is a surgical nurse. Her case is representative of one type of partnership that sometimes forms between the employer and the employee.

Linda:

"I came from a family of nine children and left home when I was sixteen to try to better myself and to help my family. I worked for T.J. for over three years and she helped me a great deal. Once Jonah was old enough for nursery school, T.J. arranged for me to take daytime classes until I graduated from high school. She also helped me find day cleaning jobs so

that I could have more money for my family and for my education. If I needed medical help, she took me to her own doctor. In a sense, T.J. showed me how to do for myself and how to determine whether or not I was getting the best value for my money. She helped me to grow up."

A Two Career Family

The Sterns are a two-parent working couple. Because June's hours are long and their youngest child is too young to stay alone, they have hired five day a week live-in help named Marta Ruiz. In addition to Marta, June also hired a college student who works from 3-5 every day driving carpools or running errands.

June:

"As an attorney with a family law practice, I feel very strongly that many of the dissolving marriages I see could have been saved with the hiring of good household help. Many woman are so angry or depressed by their lots in life, being stuck home, or holding jobs while still doing all their own housework, that they seem to prefer anger to action. They fail to pay for any help which could allow them to improve their tennis game, exercise, get away from the babies, or go to medical school. It doesn't matter. Why blame a husband for your own failure to act? For example, "Kramer vs Kramer" would have made more sense to me if Meryl Streep had tried household help as a way to find herself within her marriage or Dustin Hoffman could have hired someone from the hours of 3-6 to help parent his son so that he could keep his job. But then there would have been no movie.

I know that Dan and I make a good income and can afford any kind of household help we choose. Marta is excellent, but she started work as a housekeeper somewhere for $50 a week. Marta acts as my wife. She allows *me to do my work well, take a few hours a week between work and home for myself, and come home to a husband and children that I love."*

Dan Stern believes he was raised by household help.

"My feelings about housekeepers are very complicated. It has taken me many years with some professional psychiatric help to understand my thoughts about hired household help. I was raised by housekeepers. My mother was a professional shopper and luncheon goer. When I got married I definitely did not want my wife to hire someone to take care of the children. But times change and my wife is not the type of mother that my own mother was. I think that what we have in this household is the best of both worlds: caring parents, good careers, wonderful children and competent help."

Housekeeping as a Career

Marta Ruiz sees herself as a satisfied working woman.

Marta:

"Yes, I think you can call me a professional housekeeper. I have worked as a live-in in only two houses in the last twelve years. People know my work is good and they pay me well.

When I first came here, I knew how to clean, what to clean first, what to clean last, and what "dirty" means. But I had never seen all the appliances and cleaning products. In my country we had soap, water and a mop. A clothes washer was a large can with a hose nearby.

But the money was still uncertain; Gilbert, my husband, was often laid off. When my employers were sick, went away, or didn't have money, I was told not to come. So when one of my day jobs asked me to live-in, I thought about it for a long time and then agreed.

My husband and I shared one great wish, that our children would not have to suffer the poverty that we did. I hope that God will grant my children a good future, a good education, so that they can open new doors."

Successful Homemaker

Household help can assist all women who desire to be successful homemakers.

Sharon Brandon is a fulltime housewife, as much as she hates the term.

"I thought that by having a teaching career before Frank and I had children I would gain enough professional self esteem to happily 'retire' and enjoy raising a family. My life did not exactly work out as I thought it would. Frank was still in his residency when our oldest son, Charles, was born and I felt fairly depressed staying at home with the baby, without Frank and without the rewards of the outside world. No one cared that I made my own baby food or knitted countless baby sweaters. Then I had our daughter, Lisa, and life really began to close in on me.

Frank was doing better in his work. It seemed that he enjoyed his long office hours and his time at the hospital away from home. Who could blame him? Two whining babies could not inspire anyone. I felt like I was raising my children alone. The inequities in our lives were becoming greater and I began to feel re-

sentful. Frank was getting ahead; I was moving backwards.

Finally I couldn't take it anymore. I called Frank at the office in tears and told him that he could leave for lunch and go anywhere, any time he chose, but that one of my friends had just stopped by with a picnic basket and I could not join her for lunch because I would get too far behind in my diaper washing.

I told Frank that a girlfriend had suggested that what I needed more than a picnic lunch was a live-in housekeeper. He agreed. My girlfriend brought over her housekeeper's sister. Her name was Concha and she didn't speak a word of English. I didn't mind at all. I was so thrilled to have an extra pair of hands. We worked elbow to elbow together until she learned my routine. Now I could enjoy my babies. I could go out for lunch whenever I chose to. My resentment toward Frank began to fade because I could now enjoy being with him and sharing in his success. Concha did not stay forever. Rosario, who is with us now, won't stay forever either. But I can say this for sure, I'll never be without a housekeeper again.

I still resent that blank on forms that ask me to fill in my occupation because I hate writing that I am a housewife. But truthfully, what you are in life isn't as important as how much you like what you are doing. I enjoy my life. Together, Rosario and I run a darn good home."

Housekeeping as a Temporary Job

Rosario Valendez:

"I used to think that being a maid is the lowest form of employment. We had servants in my parents' home and I thought that I would never be able to humiliate myself to do that kind of work. But now I see that being a maid can be a decent job; it pays me well...and lets me keep my dignity.

CHAPTER TWO

Deciding to Get Help

Deciding to get help is often a difficult decision to reach. This chapter will list and explain the varied reasons that prevent people from hiring help and answer the many common reservations about household help.

"But Won't I Feel Guilty Having Someone Else Do My Housework or Childcare?"

- Maybe. Would you, as an executive, type your own letters? Paying for household help is a trading of economic services. You are paying someone to work in your home in return for time to devote to other activities. Some of these other activities could bring you a greater return on your investment of time than washing socks, not to mention greater satisfaction.
- You need not abandon your role as keeper of the home or primary nurturer for your family. You can remain in charge while you pay for assistance.
- With the many changes facing the American family today and causing changes within a woman's traditional role, it is time for many women to stop being superwomen and to begin to enjoy the benefits of paid household help.
- Some guilt is probably helpful. Guilt keeps you motivated.

Sharon Brandon:

"I used to feel guilty not cleaning right along beside my first housekeepers. But I don't anymore. I think I am an even better wife and mother now that I have help. I feel better about myself, and I have more time to do the things I want to do for my family.

I'm sure Phyllis Schafly has been employing household help for years. How else would she have time to fly all over the country speaking on the necessity of a woman's place being at home? Believe me, a woman is in her home — a paid housekeeper — not Phyllis!"

"But Aren't Servants Only For The Wealthy?"

- Yes and no. If by "servants" you mean a trained professional similar to a butler or lady's maid portrayed in films or novels, then yes, servants usually earn high salaries that only the wealthy can afford to pay.
- If, on the other hand, you are able to pay minimum wage to someone for an entry level job that entails cleaning your home and/or babysitting your children, then no, domestic help is not exclusively for the rich. In some cases the domestic help we interviewed employed household help themselves.
- *Get Help!* does not address the subject of servants for the wealthy. The text does not even use the words "servant" or 'maid" because the terms connote an imagery of servitude which can be harmful to the entire idea of hiring help. Successful women need partners or assistants, not servants.

"Who Are Household Workers? If I Cannot Afford 'Mary Poppins' or 'Jeeves the Butler,' Who Can I Afford?"

- Anybody. While you are visualizing servants for the wealthy and attempting to remove that stereotype from your mind, remove at the same time the ethnic group you see as the 'servant'. Household workers can be from any ethnic group, nationality, race, or even sex. While it is true that in southwestern cities such as Los Angeles or Dallas, some live-in housekeepers are Hispanic, anybody can serve as a housekeeper or driver or babysitter.
- One woman in Gail Sheehy's *Pathfinders* hired her mother-in-law to run the house and care for the children after the death of her husband. She offered her late husband's mother 20% of whatever she earned in return for being her household partner. The wife did not consider herself wealthy and the mother-in-law did not consider herself a servant.
- A household employee can be a student who is looking for inexpensive housing in exchange for some housework duty and wages.
- A household employee can be a neighbor — elderly, divorced, teenager, anyone on limited income who needs to stay close to home and needs to work part-time. Many new rent-a-wife businesses have been started by young mothers who charge by the hour to act as one's wife.
- A household employee may be someone else's employee whom you hire to drive, clean, or babysit for you during her free time. Some household workers are underemployed and may welcome the opportunity for extra part-time work.
- A household employee who does not speak English and is willing to live in is usually the least expensive full-time form of household help.

"But I Don't Have Room For a Live-In."

- Compare the cost of modifying your home for a live-in employee to the cost of employing a person who does not live in. Decide which is more affordable — the room modification or the higher wages of a live-out employee.

  Carefully survey your home or apartment for unused or under- used space.

- Consider the following:
  - Your den, office, or sewing room
  - Your dining room
  - Moving two children out of their separate bedrooms
  - Temporarily having the housekeeper share the baby's room

- Consider minor or major construction:
  - Opening two large back-to-back closets
  - A garage apartment with a bath
  - Converting a back service porch or laundry room
  - Dividing a large bedroom or family room
  - Adding the entire structure

- Share a housekeeper — she works days for you but spends the night, close by, in another apartment or home.

- Move.

"But I Need My Privacy."

- A household worker is usually not interested in becoming involved in your family arguments or other aspects of your personal life.
- An employee can maintain, indeed needs, privacy and you can maintain yours.
- For a live-in person, try to keep their living quarters separate from yours. The more self-contained their room is, the more they will live apart from you.

- If the job entails childcare, too much artificial separation between you and your housekeeper may make the job difficult with your children. A certain amount of closeness is needed to be effective.
- The inability to speak or understand fluent English sometimes provides privacy.

"But I Don't Speak a Foreign Language."

- So you only got a "D" in French II. This is not the same situation. Most non-English speaking housekeepers know that they can earn more money when they speak more English; most are anxious to learn. They are also anxious to keep their jobs and will try to understand your attempts at their language. If you try, you will soon communicate and will be tempted to write that old French teacher a letter in a few months.
- Purchase an English/foreign language dictionary.
- Say the same few words to your housekeeper over and over again in English.
- For a higher salary, you can specify that the person you hire speak some English.

"But Will My Children Be Able to Communicate?"

- Your child was not capable of talking for several years and you knew what he wanted then.
- Children don't really seem to have a language problem. Watch them. Before you can help them, they will have the housekeeper get them orange, not apple, juice, in the red, not the green, cup, and the "Frosted Flakes", not the "Cheerios", in the Mickey Mouse dish, not the Snoopy bowl, with low-fat milk, not the non-fat kind.

- You can teach your children and your housekeeper the words and phrases they need to communicate.
- Some people who are gone most of the day worry about the educational effect a non-English speaking employee will have on the verbal development of their child. Studies have shown that children raised in bi-lingual homes have increased verbal skills because they have learned more than one way to express themselves.
- Many families who employ non-English speaking help express pleasure because their children have learned to communicate in another language.
- If your communication concerns are directed toward how a non- English speaking person can handle an emergency situation, consult the emergency section in the Appendix. Emergency situations require quick thinking in addition to the ability to summon help. Any person left in charge of your children (including yourself) needs to be prepared to act. The ability to act under stress may be a more important attribute in an emergency situation than the ability to speak English.

"I Am Worried About My Ability to Act as a 'Boss'"

- Lots of people worry that they would feel uncomfortable or be incapable of giving orders to an employee in their home. Household employment is indeed a unique situation in that you are the sole employer for usually one employee. This might be your first experience as a supervisor and may also be the first job for your employee.

- Remember that most people in a supervisory position in any industry worry about how they function as a boss. They worry about how to direct employees, what happens if they hire incompetent employees, how will they ever know what to say to an employee when they fire them and so forth. And they make mistakes. Fear of giving directions or of making mistakes need not prevent you from trying to employ help.
- The purpose of this book is to give you all the information you may need in order to feel more comfortable as an employer. By using the information in this book and combining it with your own style and needs, you will find that you can learn to be an effective employer without ever being a "bossy" person.

"But Aren't Most Non-English Speaking Housekeepers Illegal Aliens?"

- Maybe. Some live-in housekeepers are undocumented, especially those from Mexico and Central America. Another group of women, usually from Europe, come here legally on visitor's visas but let their visas expire while they continue working in homes without legal documentation.
- At the time of this writing, you are not in legal difficulty by hiring an undocumented worker. The bill currently awaiting passage makes it illegal for an employer to knowingly hire five or more undocumented employees.
- See the Appendix section on the legal ramifications of the undocumented worker, which includes expired visas, how to obtain a green card, and the road to citizenship.

"But Aren't Household Workers One More Group of Exploited Workers?"

- Sometimes, yes.
- There are many stories about the exploited household worker. Every six months or so a newspaper article appears explaining how some person or group of workers were forced to work for nothing with the threat of physical harm or deportation used to keep them silent. Some more subtle forms of exploitation also occur, such as sponsoring a worker for legal status, a process that takes two years, and keeping that person at low level wages until he or she receives green card status.
- Over a hundred household employees were interviewed for this book and we verified all wages and working conditions. In only a few cases were workers being paid less than minimum wage. A few more had deplorable working conditions such as long hours or no vacations. Many more women simply left bad jobs as quickly as they knew they were going to be exploited. The market place often acts as a regulator of working conditions. If one place of employment does not provide fair salaries or working conditions, the employee moves on to one that does.

"I Never Feel Exploited"

Marta Ruiz (Housekeeper — age 48):

"Sometimes I don't think people here realize the true economic differences that exist between this country and my home village. I would have made much less money cleaning houses in Mexico and, yes, the cost of food and rent was also much lower. But it would have taken one emergency, one illness, and a family would be finished financially. Even mar-

riages, deaths, births were expensive. Once I worked for a family in the United States in which their little boy had to go to the hospital for an appendectomy. Sure, the family was worried and the operation cost them money. But they weren't finished as a family. In Mexico, if you only made enough to get by, one sick child who needed a doctor or the hospital would put the family in debt for the next ten years. Debts are impossible to pay off.

So how can a country exploit you if the pay is good enough to cover emergencies and to help you get ahead? Here, my husband and I make much better money. We can handle our own bad times. We can always work harder to pay off any small debt. I feel in control of my life."

GENERAL JOB CLASSIFICATIONS

Daily Cleaning Person	Errand Person
Cleaning Crew	Babysitter
Laundry Help	Driver
Cook	Help with New Baby
Seamstress	Help with a Convalescent Patient
Companion	Entertaining Help
Live-in or Live-out Housekeeper 	

CHAPTER THREE

"What Kind of Help Do I Need?" The Available Alternatives Defined

The kind of household help you may need depends upon many factors including how much you can afford to pay and how much of home care and child care you wish to delegate to a paid employee.

General Job Classification

- You may define the work to be done in your home by combining several job categories such as babysitting, cleaning and laundry and then hire one person to perform these three jobs. Or, you may hire three different people to perform each.
- With large homes, large families, or where the employers perform little home maintenance themselves, several people or full week coverage may be necessary. For example, a full time working mother who is earning a good salary may need to employ a live-in housekeeper, a driver, and a once a month cleaning crew. The hiring of additional help will assist this employer in being a successful home manager and, more important, help her keep her help.
- Pay scales listed in this chapter are general ranges; some workers charge more and some less than the range listed here. See Chapter Four, "What Will Household Help Cost?", for more wage information.

- The female pronoun is often used to describe workers in each job category because most household help is female, not because household help must or should be female. Some household workers are male.

Daily Cleaning Person

May be called Day Cleaner or Home Technician.

This person comes into your home for one day and cleans the entire home. He or she returns most items to their given places, and cleans all surfaces, counters, and furniture. He or she sweeps, washes and/or vacuums the floors. He or she cleans the bathrooms and kitchen, changes linens and makes beds, and may wash one load of dishes and one load of clothes. A day cleaner's job description does not usually include window washing, wall cleaning, oven cleaning, ironing, sewing, plant watering or any job that substantially increases a seven hour day. You may hire a person to perform only these extra jobs provided you have clearly outlined what you want done.

Hours: 6 — 7 1/2 hour day (1/2 hour lunch break included).

Pay: $4 — $12 an hour. Hours and pay depend upon many factors (See Chapter Four).

Cleaning Crew

Several people who clean your home for a specified time which may be one hour or several days depending upon the job. Cleaning crews clean the entire home and may be hired to do speciality jobs such as cleaning floors, windows, walls, garages, and so forth. Usually a cleaning crew supplies its own equipment.

Hours: Vary

Pay: $6 — $20 an hour depending upon the number of people involved.

Laundry Help

Machine washes, dries, irons, and folds laundry. May do hand washables, minor sewing and repairs.

Hours: 6 — 7 1/2 hour day, usually works on a one or two day a week basis.

Pay: $4 — $12 per hour. May have a four hour minimum.

Cook

Prepares meals. May plan, shop for groceries, and serve meals. May live-in or work dinner shift. May prepare meals in her home and deliver meals.

Hours: Usually 3 — 9 everyday, five days a week.

Pay: $5 — $15 per hour.

Driver

May drive you in your car or his or hers. May handle carpools, shopping, pick ups and deliveries. Rates and hours vary; some drivers are paid minimum wage plus expenses, some a lot more.

Hours: Vary.

Pay: $3.35 to $15 per hour, plus gas.

Seamstress

Repairs and alters clothes. May create clothes and household material goods.

Hours: Vary, may work a 6 — 7 1/4 hour day or part of a day.

Pay: $4 — $10 per hour or paid by the job, such as $5 per pant hem.

Babysitter, Au Pair, Governess

May be called babysitter, child companion, au pair, or governess. May live in or out. Duties consist of caring for the children, planning their activities, assuring their safety and well being. Duties usually do not include housekeeping. The child care person can be expected to maintain house in condition you left it and wash dishes she uses.

Hours: Vary.

Pay: $3.00 — $10/hour if they live out. May have four hour minimum, may get price break for full time or permanent part time work, or may charge per child if there are extra children.

$85 — $150 per week if live-in. For women from other countries, employer paid air fare may be expected.

Nanny

A formally trained nanny usually commands a higher salary than most forms of domestic help. A trained nanny is a person who received special training in childcare and whose duties encompass the complete care of the children. She stays with them, plans their activities, supervises their studies, maintains their rooms, their clothes, and their food. She may cook for the children but she has no other household duties unless they relate directly to the children.

Most nannies come from England and may be hired through employment agencies here or there. Word of mouth may prove effective if you know someone who employs a Nanny.

Hours: 5 — 6 day work week.

Pay: $175 — $350 a week plus room and board. Employer may also pay transportation to this country.

A Companion — For the Elderly or Handicapped

Hired help can be a wonderful alternative to a convalescent home, retirement home, state home, or your home.

A paid employee can live in or out, do light housekeeping, cooking, help her employer bathe, dress and leave the house for walks, social calls and doctor visits.

A companion will allow the handicapped or elderly to live in a private home safely and happily.

Hours: Vary.

Pay: $4—$10 per hour depending on skills. $85—$250 per week if a live-in. Employees with practical nursing experience may cost more.

Companion in a Convalescent Home

It is also possible to hire someone to help you with a disabled person in a nursing or convalescent home in addition to whatever staff is employed there. Sometimes you can hire a person who arrives just at dinner time to assist in the feeding of dinner. They can also check bedding, read or write letters, take walks, and make sure that the patient is specially cared for.

Hours: Vary.

Pay: $4—10 per hour.

Shopper/Errand Person

May run errands in her car, including grocery shopping, gift selection, mailing, etc. May be a neighbor or entrepreneur who operates a rent-a-wife business.

Hours: Vary.

Pay: $4—$25 an hour depending upon the amount of decision making and consulting time involved.

Live-In or Live-Out Housekeepers

- Maintains your home, babysits the children, and does the laundry.
- May perform any or all of the other previously mentioned tasks such as sewing, cooking, or driving.
- Each additional job classification performed by a housekeeper which requires additional skills must be paid for accordingly.

Live-Out Housekeeper:

Hours: 6 — 7 1/2 hour day. May start in late morning so as to work through dinner. May have flexible hours.

*Pay: $4 — $10 an hour or $150 — $300 a week for five day work week.

Live-In Housekeeper:

Hours: 6 — 9 hour day - 5 or 5 1/2 day work week, Monday through Friday or Tuesday through Saturday.

*Pay: $85 — $250 per week plus room and board.

Houseman

Duties are the same as a housekeeper plus heavy work, car washing, and windows.

Hours and Pay: same as housekeeper.

*pay — hourly or weekly pay scale is based upon many factors such as skill level of employee and length of work day — Please see Chapter Four for complete pay information.

Temporary Help

Any situation that temporarily upsets your routine, may require temporary help to alleviate your predicament. A day cleaner, a laundry person, a driver, someone else's housekeeper, or a temporary housekeeper could be hired for the following situations. In all cases it is advisable that you *pay more than the minimum wage* and that you *hire someone with experience.*

- **A New Baby.** Consider hiring a temporary live-in housekeeper as a good alternative to an in-law or a baby nurse. You could also hire someone's live-in or day cleaner for one to three hours a day for several weeks after you come home from the hospital with a new baby. In either case, she can prepare meals, do laundry, clean, or babysit while you rest or spend time with the older children. It helps to hire her for light cleaning several weeks before the baby is born.

Sharon Brandon:

> *"I had no real help with my first baby, Frank took a long weekend, his mother brought lunch. That was it. My doctor and all baby books I read advised me to have some kind of household help when I got home with the baby — but I didn't know where to get someone or how to do it. I even thought that a stranger in the house might be upsetting, might keep me from feeling close to my baby. The second time around, I got smart. I hired someone else's live-in to help me out.*
>
> *Before I had help I was certain that my baby had ingeniously wired the house so that anytime I sat down, a fire gong would somehow go off in his crib. When Concha came I could, for the first time, eat a dinner with my husband, nap when my baby did while Concha walked my two year old, talk for more than a minute on the phone and, in general, feel human again."*

- **A Convalescent Patient.** Again, a temporary live-in housekeeper may serve as a less expensive alternative to a registered nurse, provided that her duties are not medical but mostly housekeeping and/or driving. She too could be hired to work before or after her workday elsewhere.

- **Moving.** Hire someone for three to five days to help you move out of your old home and into your new home. She can pack, clean out the houses, unpack and ease the chaos of moving. She can watch the children so that they can participate in the move but not interfere with all the work involved.

- **House For Sale.** Hiring a cleaning person or cleaning crew to completely shine and polish a house that is on the market may increase the amount it sells for or cause it to sell faster.

- **Entertaining.** For your next party, hire someone's housekeeper or a day worker, neighbor, etc. to assist you with the preparation, serving, and clean up. You may feel like a guest at your own party.

- **Houseguests.** Having a housekeeper help with the meals, laundry, cleaning and childcare will allow you to more fully enjoy your houseguests. You may even stop Xing off the days until they leave.

- **Out-of-Town.** Hire someone when you go away and have left the children with a sitter. Whoever stays with your children while you are out of town faces the challenge of running your home while trying to care for your children. The presence of a person with childcare and cleaning experience will prove enormously helpful and be greatly appreciated.

"What Kind of Help Do I Need?"

BASIS FOR HOW MUCH HOUSEHOLD HELP COSTS

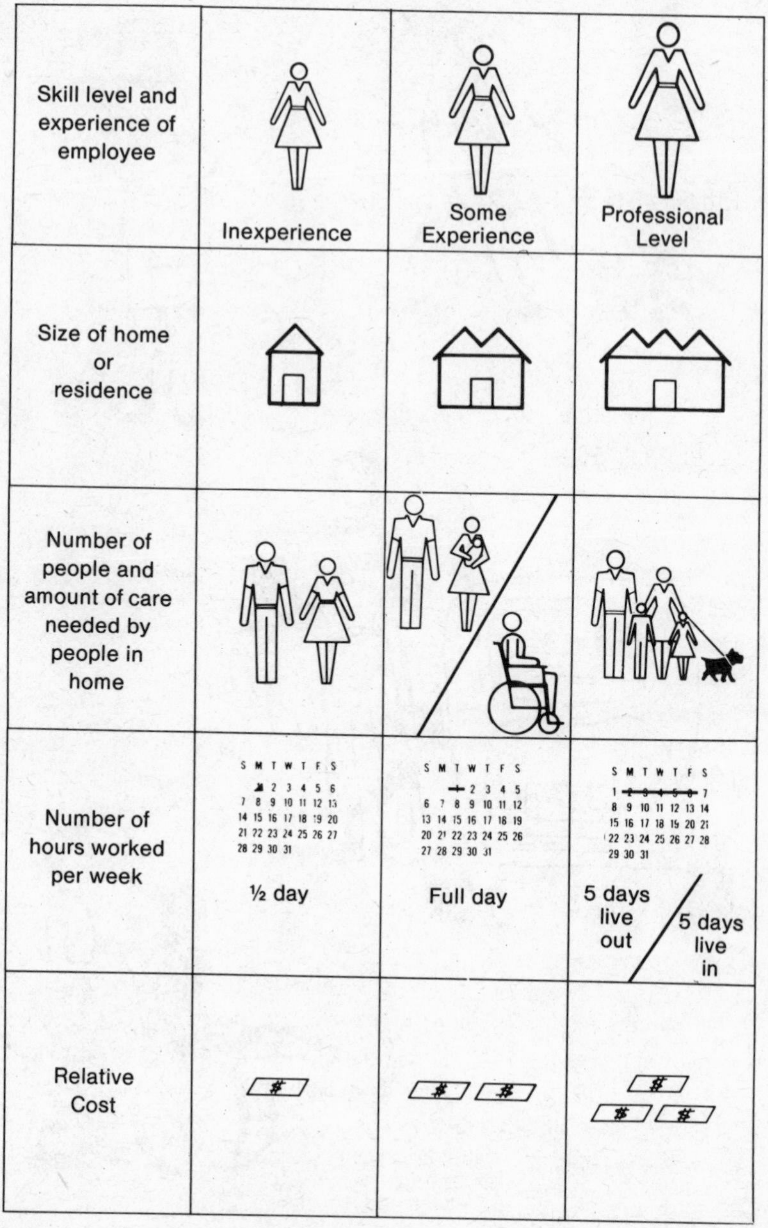

Skill level and experience of employee	Inexperience	Some Experience	Professional Level
Size of home or residence			
Number of people and amount of care needed by people in home			
Number of hours worked per week	½ day	Full day	5 days live out / 5 days live in
Relative Cost	$	$ $	$ $ $

CHAPTER FOUR

"What Does Household Help Cost?"

All wages and working conditions are based upon the idea that working in your home is as real a job as teaching school or manufacturing belts.

Starting level for most jobs is minimum wage or $3.35 an hour. But household workers are *not* covered under minimum wage laws set up by the federal government. Many states have established their own set of guidelines for domestic employees and *do* include household workers as a job classification to be paid under minimum wage. The recommendations outlined in this chapter will therefore utilize the guidelines set up by these states or will adapt to household workers those wage practices which are commonly found in other industries.

Wages For Live-Out Employees, Day Cleaners, Drivers, Etc.

- Wages for household employees who do not live in your home are based upon the numbers of hours they work, their levels of experience, their additional skills such as cooking or sewing, and the ability to speak English. Sometimes the wage is simply based on what their other employers in the same neighborhood are paying for approximately the same work.

- Most household employees at the beginning salary level earn slightly more than mimimum wage. We recommend starting at:
  - $4 an hour for inexperienced help
  - $5 to $8 an hour for an intermediate level person
  - $8 to $15 an hour for a professional, experienced, take-charge worker
- You can hire a reliable day cleaner with one to three years experience and some English for $30 a day

  Hours: 6 — 7 1/2 hours a day including 1/2 hour for lunch.
- Wages for half-day employees are usually paid at a higher hourly rate or are based upon a three to four hour minimum.
- Wages may be slightly higher if you employ a person through an agency.
- If you are hiring the same person to work in your home for two or more days a week, you may negotiate a weekly salary with this person that may be slightly less than a straight hourly figure because you are guaranteeing steady work with benefits.
- Supply and demand of household employees can alter wage rates during any economic cycle.

Wages, Hours, and Working Conditions For Live-In Workers

Again, not all states cover live-in domestic workers by wage laws or by labor guidelines. Each state may differ. The following are the hours, wages, and working conditions for live-in employees as stated by the State of California Department of Industrial Relations. It would be a good idea to follow working hours and conditions similar to these regardless of where you live.

- **Hours and Days of Work** — From California Department of Industrial Relations.

  A live-in employee shall have at least twelve consecutive hours free of duty each work day of 24 hours.

  The employee shall have at least three hours free of duty during the 12 hour work span — they need to be consecutive.

  If an employee is required to work during her three hour free time off during her twelve hour off-duty time, she shall be compensated at the rate of one and one-half times the employee's regular rate of pay.

No live in employee shall be required to work more than five days in any one work week without a day off, unless compensated at one and one-half times the employee's regular rate of pay.

- **Minimum Wages.** Every employer shall pay to each employee wages not less than $3.35 an hour for all hours worked.

  Learners, employees who have had no previous experience, may be paid not less than 85% of the minimum wage for their first 150 hours (4 weeks).

- **Meals and Lodging.** Meals, adequate and well balanced, may be subtracted from the minimum wage at the rate of $5.05 per day.

  Lodging means living accommodations that are decent, adequate, and sanitary. Lodging may be credited as part of minimum wage at the rate of $5.20 per day for a room for one person and $2.60 a day for a room that must be shared.

What Does This Really Mean?

- California State regulations mean essentially that if you employ a beginning level person and if she works an eight hour day, you should pay her $3.35 an hour or $26.80 a day. You subtract the cost of room and board which the state computes at $10.25 a day, for a minimum daily rate of $16.55.
- Weekly pay for an eight hour day, five days a week, should be, therefore, $82.75.
- If she is new to the country and/or new to living-in as a housekeeper, she may be paid 85% of this amount for the first month, or $70 a week as a training period.
- A day longer than eight hours requires a higher hourly rate of pay. A day longer than nine hours requires time and a half for hours in excess of nine hour day, as does the sixth day of a six-day work week.

The Current Wage Rate For Live-In Employees

Throughout the country, the weekly pay scale for any live-in worker is based upon the following:

- Level of experience, how many years worked in homes, and competence level at each household task.
- Ability to speak English.
- Ability to perform additional tasks beyond housecleaning and babysitting, such as driving, grocery shopping, meal planning, etc.
- General salary range for that particular geographical area.

LEVEL		WEEKLY PAY
1. Beginning level	New in the country, little or no English, no paid cleaning experience.	$85–$95
2. Intermediate level	2-5 years experience, English (or fluent English, but no paid experience).	$100–$140
3. Professional	6 or more years experience, good English, driver's license and/or meal planning and cooking, or other special training.	$150–$250

"What Else Determines Wages?"

Basically, any factor that increases the amount of time necessary to work in your home affects the wage level. Work done in your home that requires more than a nine hour work day should be paid for at a higher hourly rate. Consider:

- The size of your home.
- The number of people residing in your home.
- The special needs of those people such as elderly, disabled, twins.
- The ages of the children.
- The amount of time adults are home. Their presence or absence can affect the amount of responsibility given to the housekeeper.
- The type of extra skills a housekeeper may have such as cooking, sewing, or driving.
- The access to your home; employment far from transportation may require higher pay because your employee must pay extra for private transportation.
- The amount and regularity of supplemental help you may hire, such as window washers, floor polishers, and so forth.
- In some areas of the country where there is a larger supply of household workers, wages are higher in the affluent section of the city. Realistically, these higher wages are based upon the employer's ability to pay and the assumption that the homes are larger and require longer hours. Some communities have a community wage standard. Learn your community's wage rates from your neighbors or from a local household employment agency.

Paid and Unpaid Days Off

In other industries, paid benefits are not always granted to minimum wage level employees — we acknowledge this economic fact. But we believe that employers who include paid benefits, such as paid vacations and sick leave, will have a better chance of cutting down on employee turnover.

- **Paid Vacations**

  For live-in employees, we suggest you provide one week paid vacation after one year of employment. Two weeks paid vacation after two or more years of employment is generally recommended.

  For live-out employees, provide one day's vacation for each number of days of the week worked in your home. If a person works for you on Tuesdays, for example, grant one paid Tuesday off a year.

- **Paid Holidays — For Live-In Employees**

  Provide six to nine paid days a year. Yes, we know that July 4th is not a holiday for other nationalities, but it may be a time when their friends and family are home from work. Most employers also give Christmas, New Year's Eve and New Year's Day, Good Friday, Labor Day, Thanksgiving and the employee's birthday off with pay.

- **Paid Sick or Personal Business Days**

  Three to five a year. You should be notified in advance if possible. Again, a day worker needs one paid day for each day of the week worked.

- **Unpaid Days Off**

  If an employee needs more than these days off, try trading services, such as a Friday off with pay for working on a non-regular work day without extra pay. Days in excess of what is listed can be given, without pay.

- **Extra Pay**

  Extra pay is given at more than the hourly rate for any extra service such as:

- Working on a normally paid day off such as a holiday.
- Parties.
- Overnight house guests.
- Home remodeling — or any condition that can add to the normal work day.

Payroll Record Keeping

- For those of you who desire to follow the correct payroll record keeping procedures, the next several pages will briefly outline what is meant by payroll record keeping, employment taxes, payroll deductions, and the like.
- Employers are required to keep payroll records, pay employment taxes (such as Social Security), and deduct income tax withholding, and other taxes from employee wages.
- All employment taxes are considered part of the cost of employment. They are additions to the employee's actual wages, both in dollar amounts and in terms of time devoted to bookkeeping and report making. Raises for employees will usually entail an increase in the dollar amount paid to each employee and an increase in your employment taxes.
- You cannot choose to participate in selective payroll reporting to either the state or federal government without being liable for all legal employer requirements. For example, you cannot contribute to Social Security on behalf of your employee and choose to ignore unemployment tax.

To Participate in Federal and State Employment Tax Programs

I. Obtain a Federal Employer Identification Number (EIN) from the Internal Revenue Service; you may apply by mail. We suggest that you also request from the Internal Revenue Service the Employer's Tax Guide which contains a great deal of useful information for the first time employer. As an employer, you will be required to file Form 940 to report Federal employer contributions and payroll deductions and to make deposits based upon the size of your payroll.

2. Obtain a State Employer Identification Number in order to make State related payroll deductions, pay State mandated employment taxes, and file State Quarterly Reports of Wages, etc.

3. Require your employee to obtained a Social Security Identification Number (SSA) so that they can fill out a W4 form for you.

4. Purchase from a stationary store a book of blank record keeping forms called "Statement of Earnings and Deductions." These forms help you keep accurate records and fulfill the requirement in some states that you give your employee a copy of deductions taken out of each paycheck.

Employment Taxes and Payroll Deductions

Depending on the actual amount of gross wages you pay your employee(s), you will be required to remit some or all of the following:

- **Social Security**, or FICA is a federal government mandated insurance plan that provides monthly benefit payments in the event of disability or death; it is paid for equally by employer and employee.

  - This tax is currently equal to 13.4% of the total (gross) wages; 6.7% is taken out of the employee's paycheck and 6.7% is contributed by the employer.

- The total amount deducted (employee) and contributed (employer) is remitted periodically to the Federal Government.

- **Federal or State Personal Income Tax Withholding**. Income tax withholding amounts are deducted from the employee's pay based on the amount of pay and the number of employee deductions. These amounts are remitted periodically to the federal and state governments. The Bureau of Internal Revenue provides federal income tax withholding information and forms.

- **State Disability.** If your state requires such a plan, the contribution is usually deducted from the employee's pay. New York requires disability insurance for employers of fours or more workers.

- **Unemployment Insurance** is normally employer paid. The employer is given a rate of about 3.5% depending upon the number of claims filed against any one employer. As an employer, you may have to pay both State and Federal Unemployment Insurance taxes.

- **Workers' Compensation**. Workers' compensation plans provide medical benefits for job related illness or injury and sometimes reimburse lost pay due to injury on the job. It is possible your homeowner's insurance policies contains workers' compensation coverage for any employee in the home. Check your policy. Coverage is strongly recommended for all employees in your home.

  In New York State, workers' compensation is a legal requirement for employers of household workers who work for one employer 40 hours or more a week. Workers' compensation is available from private insurance carriers and also in New York and some other states, from the state insurance fund. The coverage for a full time person (40 hours or more a week) is about $130 a year. Coverage for a part time employee is not mandatory in New York but is recommended.

Income Reporting for Undocumented Foreign Employees

- As a practical matter, many employers of undocumented household workers do not report earnings or pay into Social Security plans because the employee is not here legally, would never receive these benefits, and does not pay income taxes.
- Some workers, without legal papers, have purchased false social security cards. A false social security card helps an employee open a bank account, participate in some government programs, obtain a factory job, get mail at the post office, etc. (To protect yourself, you may make contributions under the name of this false number, but we don't really see the point).
- You are legally responsible to pay social security on those people who are here with legal papers, whether they desire this coverage or not.

Voluntary Payroll Deduction and Contribution Plans

- You and your employee may investigate and enroll in various voluntary insurance plans.

- You may establish health insurance, dental insurance, and retirement plans for your employee.

- Payments into these plans may be contributed by the employer, deducted from the employee's take home pay, or a combination of both.

- Obtain written permission from each employee before you remit money to any of these plans.

- Voluntary payroll deductions which you and your employee have established do not always require an employer or employee identification number.

- If you are employing domestic employees through an agency, the agency may be assuming payroll deduction responsibilities. Check with your agency.

Pay Period

- Every week.
- In cash (by check if your employee prefers or you are making deductions).
- If you must pay monthly, remember that a month equals 4.3 weeks so it is necessary to consider all the days of employment. In some states it is illegal to pay any less often than twice a month.
- Many housekeepers from other countries send money home. If they are only paid once a month and have only Mondays or one business day off to do their personal business, sending money home and meeting their other financial obligations is very difficult.

Raises

- We suggest that you raise a live-in employee $5 a week after the first week or so of employment provided you are both satisfied with each other and the work.
- Live-in housekeepers make more money by gaining experience. If the employee began at an inexperienced salary level, raise that person $5 a week every six months for several years as recognition for experience.
- For household help other than live-in or for live-in household help who begin work at a higher salary level, decide with that employee at the time of employment a percentage salary increase rate that is amenable to you both. You may use federal inflation rates, federal employee salary raise rates or any cost of living index that is applicable. These percentage increase rates can range from 0% to about 15% a year.
- Just like any major employer, you may increase benefits in addition to salary and decide jointly how often the two of you will re-negotiate the entire package.

- A raise should be granted to either a live-in or live-out person for additional work responsibilities such as a new baby, or starting dinner, and for the acquisition of new skills. If you are increasing job duties, you need to increase salary. Raises are measures of increased experience, loyalty, and recognition of a job well done. Raises are very important to your employee.
- If you do not want to give an employee a raise because he or she is not doing an adequate job, try to improve performance or terminate employment. Don't use money as punishment.

"Money Isn't Everything"

So said Gina, a live-in housekeeper with three years experience, about the job she just quit.

> *"I took the last job because the pay was $140 a week, a lot more than I had ever been paid. The house was small and the family only had one son who was gone most of the day. After I was hired, I found out that the workday at that house was to start at 6:30 in the morning. They wanted coffee in bed. And they kept giving me orders like some slave until sometimes 11:30 at night. Counting on your fingers, that's a 17 hour day. I'd take less money to work in a home where the workday was shorter, where I got to make some decisions, and where I was treated like a good person."*

CHAPTER FIVE

How to Afford Household Help

What someone can afford to spend on household help is a relative matter. By determining your exact income and expenses, you can figure out what you can and cannot afford.

Add Up What You Are Spending Now

To determine whether or not you can afford live-in help full time, add up what you are already spending per week for household cleaning, laundry service, childcare, and transportation for these services. Many women are surprised about how much they are spending.

Here is an example of the weekly expenses for someone who could probably afford live in help and would undoubtedly be receiving more for her money.

Wednesday cleaning woman	$35.00
Saturday night babysitter	9.00
Laundry, such as shirts and sweaters at cleaners	10.00
Weekday babysitting	15.00

TOTAL	$69.00
Beginning level non-English speaking, live-in housekeeper	$85.00

- For sixteen dollars more a week she could have continuous babysitting, a clean home, dinner dishes done, laundry clean and an order to her home and to her life that she can depend on.
- In determining what you are really spending and what you really can afford to spend, it is important to add the incidental monetary expenses to the basic cost of your household services. A live-in employee's salary is both the cash that you pay her and the food and room costs that you pay *for* her. She may also use the telephone and electricity, and often makes more use of cleaning supplies.
- Household employees who do not speak English and are willing to live in are usually the least expensive full-time form of household help.

Affording Part Time Help

- You may not be able to afford household help on a full-time basis; you may need to start out with hourly help.

  - At approximately $3.35 an hour decide how many hours of help you can afford per week. Could you do without something else in order to have help?

  - Expending money for help in the home need not be a permanent expense. You could hire someone for a month or so and then decide whether the paid assistance has been financially and psychologically beneficial.

Careful Spending

Affording household help like any other expenditure requires careful planning and sometimes salary negotiations. Even if you are not spending anything already on household help and are just beginning to employ a home worker, you may find the following suggestions of assistance in prudent money management.

Helpful Ways to Save Money

- State the salary range you can afford *after* you have determined whether or not a prospective employee would like the job you are offering.

- Do not rely on a prospective employee's knowledge of salary ranges or working conditions. Your prospective employee may understand only that her cousin is paid $50.00 a day to watch a dog. Many employees remember and quote to you the highest wage associated with the least work — of course.

- Show your interviewee the chart on page 51 which explains how salaries are calculated.

- If your base salary is on the low end of the wage scale, consider offering extras which may make your job better than others who may pay more. Some ideas are:

  - vacation and sick pay
  - two extra evenings off a month
  - a raise system that will be based upon raises you receive in your job
  - a free room or apartment for relatives

- Be willing to begin employing this person immediately. Point out the advantage of starting with you tomorrow versus maybe getting a job up the street for more money in six weeks.

- Make your home as efficient a work place as possible. Use the suggestions from chapter eight on organization, storage, professional cleaning, supplies and so forth. Remember that time is money and the less time and effort it takes to run your home efficiently, the less it will cost you to hire help.

  Your prospective employee may appreciate the importance you have placed upon organization, efficiency and her role in your home.

- If you are willing to spend time training an inexperienced worker, you can usually save money by hiring this type of person.

- What a friend or neighbor pays for household help need not dictate your starting salary. Some employees are paid substantially more than recommended but may be working long shifts with many responsibilities. Sometimes a high salary is merely an employer status symbol and has little to do with anything except an ability to pay.
- Finally remember that with household help or with any kind of personal service type of employment, you don't always get what you pay for. With careful spending, you may get more.

We had two friends who lived next door to each other, each with three small children, and a new baby. The one neighbor paid over $600 a week for a live-in housekeeper, a driver, a day cleaning person, and a baby nurse. The other paid one person $90 a week to run an efficient home and help with the baby. This one employee performed all the same duties as the four employees next door during an eight hour time span.

TWO WORKING WOMEN

Alternative Ways to Afford Help

If you cannot afford the standard base salary for an employee, you can work out an alternative plan, provided the plan is *completely outlined, is mutually understood, stays within the minimum wage and maximum working hours*, and *provides the employee with a way to meet his or her economic goals.*

1. Find the Employee Extra Work.

Employ live-in help, pay less than the appropriate weekly rate and find this employee enough extra work to make up at least the difference.

The responsibilities with other employers are private. Do not get involved as a go-between.

If your employee is living with you, you are still financially responsible for additional expenses such as toiletries, paid days off, and the like.

Your employee could do:

- Day cleaning in another home as many days as necessary. You usually would not subtract any more than $15 per day from the weekly wage for this day out of your home.
- Work a shortened work day in your home and clean an apartment or an office in the afternoon or find babysitting, sewing, or catering jobs in the neighborhood. Babysitting for others could be on a regular basis and can be done in your home if you desire.

2. Share an Employee.

You could find one to five friends or co-workers who would be willing to hire one person to work for all of you. This employee could clean, cook, sew, babysit, drive, or perform whatever service you need.

- Keep the rules and regulations simple. All employers must agree on wages, hours, expectations; and everyone handles his or her own problems individually.
- We know three examples where sharing an employee worked out fine for everyone.

  - Three working women hired one young housewife as a driver for their children so that all the children could attend a certain school and be part of two after school activities in other parts of the city. The driver earned $6 an hour and each woman paid $2 an hour for the driving service.

  - One woman who was just starting her medical internship hired a non-English speaking housekeeper to care for her young baby but could only afford $65 a week. She found another neighbor who was willing to pay $30 a week to the housekeeper for babysitting her toddler four mornings a week. The housekeeper then made $95.00 a week.

  - One enterprising housekeeper organized a produce and laundry co-op. She would drive to the produce mart in center city once a week and purchase fresh fruits and vegetables in bulk at reduced rates and deliver the produce to five families. Each family paid $8 a week (plus the costs of food and laundry) for the delivery services. Both services took this housekeeper about 3-4 hours each week — so she made $40 a week for four hours work.

3. Room and Board Exchange

- Provide room and board for a person who is employed full time elsewhere. Her duties in your home are to help you in the evenings and/or Saturdays. Having someone work part time for you in exchange for room and board can be a complicated arrangement to set up but, if hours and responsibilities are clearly defined, it can work. Remember that room and board is worth about $10 a day, so a worker who works more than two to three hours per day for you must get a salary in addition to room and board.

Ellie, a former neighbor, found a job after her divorce. But she didn't know what to do about finding someone to care for her young daughter while she worked at a medium paying job. She asked Lillian, the day worker who cleaned the house next door, to help her find a person who could move in with her and care for her little girl from 3 p.m. to 6 p.m. every day. Lillian took the job herself, continued to work at her day cleaning jobs, and lived on with Ellie and her daughter, Sarah, for six years. Lillian moved out last year to get married and just recently had a baby daughter of her own. She named her Ellie.

4. Trade Services

- Trade a talent or service of yours with someone who can provide the household help you need.

Tax Credit for Child and Dependent Care Expenses

In determining whether or not you can afford live-in help, you may wish to consider or calculate any federal income tax credit you may be entitled to for employing household help

Do check with an accountant or Internal Revenue Service for current and accurate information. The determination of the tax credit and eligibility is rather complicated. Basically, the rules for the tax credit are:

- You must be paying at least half the cost to maintain a household.
- You (and your spouse, if applicable) must be gainfully employed or looking for work.
- Your dependents must be "qualified persons", including children under fifteen, disabled dependents, etc.
- You must keep records of all your dependent care expenses including payroll record keeping requirements for wages paid. Your employee must provide you a social security account number and you must make payroll deductions and pay employment taxes.
- Wages paid to household employees for purposes other than direct dependent care also may be included in completing the tax credit because a cleaning person, cook, or driver can be involved in the care of your child, or other dependent such as a handicapped spouse.
- Check federal income tax information form 2441 for complete rules, regulations, and percentage of tax credit allowed.

The actual amount of tax credit is a sliding scale based on your income, your tax, dependent care expense, and whether you have one or two or more qualifying dependents. The tax credit can vary from as low as -0- to $1,440 per year reduction in income tax liability.

Subtle Financial Considerations

- Live-in help offers many subtle financial benefits. Some working mothers are limited by their childcare or children's school hours as to the amount of work they can accomplish and the amount of times they can stay late. Many times, the working mother is at a disadvantage because she does not have the time to go for that meeting after work, take that long lunch break with an important client, stay on until nine to get a mailing out. Live-in help can free her to earn more money by not only allowing her to work longer hours, but also by allowing her to be part of the team, to socialize, and join her fellow workers, male or childless, when off the clock business decisions are made.

- Household help may subtly increase a husband's earning power by making it more pleasurable for his wife to participate in his work.

- Household help can improve the quality and frequency of leisure activities and thereby help one feel more productive in general.

- There are many other ways in which a household worker can either save money or increase an employer's earning potential. These benefits rely on individual circumstances to be calculated accurately.

CHAPTER SIX

Interviewing and Hiring

"How Do I Find Someone?"

- Word of mouth. Call a friend or anyone you know with household help, including drivers, day cleaners, or gardeners. Call someone who employs a person you like and whose work you admire. If they don't know of anyone looking for work, ask them to spread the word that you are looking for someone. Describe for them the position, salary, and working conditions you are offering. (Never, however, attempt to lure away a satisfied employee of a friend).
- Call religious organizations in your neighborhood or other neighborhoods. Many times they place household workers.
- Post signs in your neighborhoods or at schools, churches, and retirement centers.
- Place a classified ad in the newspaper including foreign language publications (they will usually translate your ad).
- Call a reputable, bonded, domestic employment agency.
- Call local schools and colleges — they may suggest a student looking for work.
- After you have made at least five phone calls, you can expect results in two to fourteen days.

Why Word of Mouth?

Word of mouth, especially through a neighbor's employee is perhaps the most reliable and satisfactory way to find an employment candidate for the following reasons:

1. When you hire through friends, you join a network of employers and employees who may have a better knowledge of you, your employee, and domestic employment in general.

2. Because your neighbor's employee would know the person she recommended to you, she could serve as a reliable reference, trainer, interpretor, and problem solver. This support is not always possible if hiring through a classified ad or agency.

3. Your neighbor's employee can serve as a form of emergency assistance. Because she and/or her employer are familiar with your situation, she can help call ambulances, other neighbors, or whomever in the case of accidents, illnesses, or injuries to someone in your home. She can also help find replacements or substitutes if your employee is sick or unable to work.

4. Word of mouth hiring may also help you obtain a highly recommended and highly paid employee who may choose to work for you for less than his/her usual salary because *you* have been recommended as an employer or because your home is closer to that of a friend or relative.

Placing Ads

- In writing your own sign or newspaper ad, it is important that you be as specific as you can.

- If you want a part-time childcare person, advertise that your job is part time — but that it is permanent. Describe what you are looking for, such as "energetic person to care for active two year old, four hours a day, four days a week; must drive."

- You may want to place your newspaper ads in smaller neighborhood papers to narrow the number of responses and to try to locate a local person.

- If you are looking for a college student — to live in or to drive, for example, place these ads in the college newspaper, with the college employment office, and the housing departments. You can also place ads with specific academic departments such as the early childhood education department or the foreign student exchange department.

- Be ready to screen most people responding by telephone.

- Keep a notebook for writing down the names and telephone numbers of people you want to call back for interviews.

"What About Calling an Agency?"

Yes, you can call a domestic employment agency or cleaning service. Tell them what skills you want, the size of your home and family, and how much you are willing to pay. Keep in mind:

- Most agencies screen the prospective employees and provide several candidates with references for you to interview. Most employment agencies are fairly reliable.
- If you are looking for an experienced person and are willing to pay more than a beginning level salary (over $125 a week or $40 a day), an employment agency can usually find an employee for you. Most professional level workers seek new jobs through agencies.
- The charges for an agency or cleaning service vary. Some agencies charge you a fee which is equal to an employee's weekly or monthly salary.
  Some agencies charge you a weekly fee or a percentage fee (10% — 20%) of a month's salary which drops off after six months or so of employment.
- Most agencies include a guaranteed replacement for up to three months if neither you nor your employee is satisfied with the employment.
  Some agencies will provide a monitoring service for you in that they will guarantee to replace a housekeeper immediately if you are in a situation that cannot tolerate lost work days.
- But agencies' quoted weekly salaries are often slightly higher than what you could negotiate for yourself if you hire through friends.
- If you are looking for a beginner level person, an agency can usually do no better in finding you qualified prospectives than you can do yourself through asking friends.

Describe Your Job

- Before you begin the interview, establish for yourself the wages and working conditions you are willing to offer. Express to her during the interview what her wages and working conditions will be, but leave room for negotiation. Describe your family and your family's general routine.

- Outline first to yourself, and then to her, what your role will be and what hers will be.

- After interviewing her, adjust your package according to the experience and skills of the prospective employee.

How To Interview

- Arrange to meet any prospective employees at a time and place that is convenient *for them*.

- A prospective employee might be able to be driven to your home.

- It is not necessary or recommended that you go to where they are currently living. The prospective employee needs to prove that she can get close to your home, but you need to be considerate of any transportation and language difficulties she may have.

- When language is going to be a problem, it is necessary to interview through an interpreter who is a friend of yours or of the prospective employee.

What To Ask

1. What is your name?

2. How old are you?

3. Where are you from (if not from the United States), and how long have you been in this country?

4. Why are you interested in housework?

5. What was your last job and why are you looking for work now?

6. Are you married?

7. Do you have children? How old are they? Where are they?

8. Where and with whom do you live?

9. What was your past salary and working conditions?

10. Do you like working with children (elderly, handicapped, etc.)?

11. How would you handle problems with the children, such as finding them playing with matches.

12. What are your special skills?

13. What kind of work in the house do you like the least? What work do you like the most?

14. How much school were you able to finish here or in your own country?

15. How will you get to and from work?

16. Do you smoke?

What To Look For

- Someone who wants and needs a job. You do not want to hire someone who needs temporary housing, a place to learn English, a home closer to her boyfriend, a chance to visit Chicago, or wherever you live. You want a person whose primary motivation is to work and to earn money.
- Someone whose experience, maturity, willingness to help, skills, and personality most closely meet your needs and ability to pay.
- Acceptable responses to the questions you asked in the interview.
- A smile, but remember that she may be petrified.
- A neat and clean appearance.
- Some display of affection towards children. You may wish to have one of your children around to see whether the prospective employee reaches out for him. Most children do not respond to this first contact, but don't cross her off simply because your child was not initially thrilled.
- References. For us, if she is new to this country, friends and relatives of our prospective employee serve as her references. We try to find these people.
- Some stability — a reasonable number of previous jobs, schools, marriages, and residences.
- An understanding on her part of the nature of her employment.

What To Ask References

- If working for you is this person's first job, try to find character references for her through employers of her friends and relatives. Ask them to verify the information she gave you.
- For students, try to find neighbors or school references.
- If your prospective employee has worked before at any job, ask for an employment history and call these references.
- Check the dates of employment — did she work for them as long as she said, do the stated salary and working conditions, as well as the reason for leaving, match those stated by the former employer?
- Inquire as to what the duties were and how they were performed.
- Try to ascertain the needs and priorities of her former employers and decide whether you have similar needs. Very often a former employer will tell you that their help never cleaned the kitchen and what they meant was that the kitchen was clean, the dishes washed, the floors scrubbed, but the inside of the cabinets had not been washed down that week.
- What were her childcare duties and how did she perform them?
- How reliable, honest, and loyal was she.
- References are a must if you are hiring through an agency or through a newspaper ad. When you hire through a friend, references are helpful but not as crucial.

Assessing the Information

The interview need not be lengthy. It is important that the questions are answered by the prospective employee. If he or she speaks English, that's not a problem. If they do not, you should make every effort to communicate your questions to the prospective employee and to get a reply directly from them. "Friends" who come to help with the interview might be getting a kick-back from the candidate so their answers may reflect an eagerness for immediate employment.

Household workers know what you are looking for and often are anxious to work. The truth is often stretched to make the interviewee more desirable so take note of the following answers:

- Age: In order to allay our cultural biases about one's age being an accurate indication of one's experience and ability to work, a prospective household employee may alter her age. She might be 15, 16 or 17 years old (one girl we once interviewed was only thirteen years old.)

  A seventeen year old girl, however, in her own country may already have two children. A young interviewee may be very experienced, hard-working and responsible.

  If a woman says that she is 45, she could be over 50. In fact, a 55 year old woman may have grown grandchildren and may now be looking for a home she can serve lovingly. Because of her stability, she may suit your needs perfectly.

- Time in this Country: If residency in this country is given as one year, it could actually mean anytime longer than one week. However, a housekeeper who is newly arrived may work out fine.

- Marital Status: "Married" may mean living with a boyfriend. Marital status should make no difference in anyone's overall performance. Women's rights groups have struggled a long time to strike marital and pregnancy possibilities from hiring prerequisites.

- Literacy: Whether or not an employee can read may be difficult to ascertain. Some women seeking domestic employment have had little or no schooling, indeed, often are not literate. It has been our experience, and that of the employers we've interviewed, that lack of formal education can have little relationship to a prospective employee's ability to function in your home.

Not Sure?

Don't be desperate or intimidated, expecially if you are interviewing through an agency and receive a sales pitch. If you are not at least ninety percent convinced, you can try the following suggestions. But remember, if the prospective employee is not currently employed, he or she will continue to look for work while you are trying to reach a decision.

- Use a Sunday as a trial day if she is already employed. Or try a time that both of you can be at your home, such as a Saturday night.
- Hire her for several days toward the end of the week with the clear understanding that it is to be a trial period for you both.

Rosario:

"My Uncle Eduardo prepared me for my first interview. He told me what the lady was going to ask and what he was going to answer. He was going to tell her that I was 22, even though I was 18, because he said Americans don't like to leave their children with teenagers. He said that I was experienced at cleaning houses; my aunt had taken me to her job one day. And he was going to say that housework was all I knew or ever wanted to do. I never did housework at home. He told my prospective employer not to let me go to school because I didn't need an education. He even started my salary lower than I expected to be paid. Starting my life in this country under these lies bothered me, but what could I do? Eduardo was charging me to stay at his house. He took $40 dollars for getting me the job, was going to charge me $20 a week for driving me there and back, and even charged my first employer $40 for an employment fee. When I could afford to, I told her the truth and she helped me get rid of my association with Eduardo."

CHAPTER SEVEN

Working and Living Conditions

Remember your first day on a new job when you sat with that ever grinning personnel manager and filled out those forms, got to go over a tiny employee handbook, and were then given a tour of the offices?

The employee whom you now have hired needs to go through that same first day experience in which they fill out vital information, receive a list of the new job benefits and company (or house) rules, and are then given a tour of the work place.

How to Start the First Day of Employment

- Obtain the following information: full name (we know employers who, to this day, don't know their employee's last name). Also obtain an address, a home or weekend telephone number, and the names and telephone numbers of local friends and relatives. You may also wish to have the names and addresses of family out of the country if your employee is not from the United States. For legal residents, obtain a Social Security number.

- Go over your initial employment agreement with your new person and ascertain whether all wages and working conditions are agreeable. There may be a few working conditions that either of you may have to re-negotiate as the job progresses, but begin your first days in tentative agreement as to salary, days, off, length of work day, and so forth.
- Introduce your employee to your family. We all go on a first name basis — but decide for yourself how you wish to be addressed. Do not Americanize her name.
- Walk this person through your home and yard showing her the rooms of the house, closets, cabinets, additional exits, and any alarm or detector systems. You may need to familiarize her with the alarm systems' workings so that she will not accidently set them off.
- Show this person all telephones. Identify one telephone as one which has emergency phone numbers written out beside it. You may wish to practice dialing one emergency. Make sure your full name, phone number, and address are written on your emergency phone number list. Any fire or police department dispatcher will need to know the location of your emergency.
- Explain any other general rules and regulations of your home such as telephones not to answer, doors that are not to be opened, dogs that will bite anyone, etc.

Accouterments Provided —

Bedroom for Live-In Employee

Have ready a bedroom-living room for a live-in employee. This room is best located away from your bedroom and should contain the following:

1. Bed with extra blankets and change of linens.
2. Bureau and/or closet with hangers.

3. Soap, deodorant, and other toiletries. You may wish to continue to supply toiletries because a live-in employee must carry her personal items back and forth to your home each week.

4. Towels, washcloths, and an extra set of both.

5. Television — need not be color but should be able to receive foreign language station if your employee desires.

6. Clock with alarm.

7. Mirror.

8. Telephone.

9. Extra niceties to include are a radio, table for eating and writing, extra chairs, and decorative accessories.

Meals

Several household workers voiced strong complaints about the food that was either not available or was noticeably different (cheaper and less abundant) than the food for the rest of the family.

- Food should be the same as for the rest of the family — nutritious, abundant, and accessible. Your housekeeper may not be thrilled by having to go on your family's latest fad diet.
- Ask your employee to let you know whether she wants special ethnic foods. Tell her she is welcome to anything in the refrigerator unless you instruct otherwise.
- Most housekeepers fix their own lunch and breakfast and, if not hired to cook, eat what you cook for dinner or cook for themselves. You must specify which leftovers you intend to use, otherwise, the extra piece of chicken will be her lunch.
- Day workers are provided with lunch, coffee, and soft drinks.

Where Does an Employee Eat?

- Most housekeepers prefer to eat in their rooms or in the kitchen.
- If they are new arrivals to this country, they may like to join you for a family get acquainted dinner during the first week in your home.
- Who eats dinner with you is really a good indication of who you consider family and who you consider outside help.
- People we interviewed had differing reactions:

Mary Beth:

"Of course we eat all our meals together. Delia doesn't understand a word of English but I translate some of the conversation for her. Each night we sit down to dinner, hold hands around the table and say our thank yous."

We asked Delia where she would choose to eat her dinner.

Delia:

"They insist that I have dinner with them every night, which is nice for them I guess. But, really, my manners aren't so good and I don't understand what they are saying. I would prefer to eat alone in my room and watch television. At least then maybe I could sit still for a half-hour and not have to jump up every time the baby spills something or get things that I forgot to put on the table."

"Am I Responsible for Her Dinner When We Go Out?"

Yes, in that the food is to be available. You are not responsible for dinner preparation. We have had housekeepers tell us that there was no food in the house if the family ate out or that they were handed two eggs to fry for themselves for dinner.

"What About Uniforms?"

- Your choice; you purchase.
- Sometimes uniforms protect a limited wardrobe, however, they can be degrading; ask your employee.

Transportation

- Avoid personally transporting household workers.
- For day workers, add bus or carfare to their pay.
- You may call the bus or train company and get the numbers, routes, and times.
- If an employee is new to the country or unfamiliar with your neighborhood, pick her up and drive her to your home for the first week. Drive along the bus route so that she can get an idea of the distance to your home and can remember the landmarks along the way.
- If you can afford to risk a foul-up for the second week, let her try to get to your home by herself. Make sure she has your phone number and knows how to pay the correct change for bus and phone. She may need a slip of paper with your address, phone number, bus route and times.
- If your house is too far away from the bus route, pick the nearest stop with a pay phone and have her call you. Don't set a time to meet her there; the buses are not always reliable.
- She may be paying for rides to your home because it is inaccessible. If this is the case, you need to pay for transportation.

"Health Checks?"

We recommend a health check-up by your physician or a nearby clinic as soon as you know that you are going to retain an employee, especially a live-in employee. The check-up need not be elaborate, but should include a tuberculosis skin test and perhaps a chest x-ray. Drivers need vision and hearing tests. The health check-up is at your expense; it is for your protection.

Telephone — Employee Personal Use

Rosario, at her first live-in job:

> *"I was not prepared for the feeling of isolation I had at not being able to speak English. It made me feel like I was paralyzed. I couldn't talk or hear for entire weeks. I missed home so much that I cried myself to sleep."*

- Telephone use permits your housekeeper to socialize. We believe it is a must. Imagine how isolated you would feel if you were unable to communicate with anyone.
- For a live-in employee, install a separate phone line in her room. Ask for the numbers she frequently calls and have these prefixes covered under the extended service plan of the telephone company.
- Outline a few rules for telephone usage in your home: No telephone use from 8 a.m. to 2 p.m. during work hours; no long distance calls made or received collect without your permission. You may offer to pay for one or two long distance calls a year. Deduct any gross violation.
- Choose a new phone with a separate ring so that it is distinct from your phone.
- Change the number of the housekeeper's phone if you are going through a lot of housekeepers so that they don't reverse charges to you after they have left your employment because they are angry with you.

- This extra line and service should cost $12 — $20 a month. You can add an extension and use the additional line yourself.
- You may omit installing a live-in housekeeper's line if you wish, but telephone problems were such a commonly mentioned source of friction that the additional phone line could save a lot of aggravation.
- To ascertain whether she is spending too many work hours on the phone, check your bill and note the times that calls are being made.
- Long distance calls can be heartbreaking. Try to be as fair as possible, but they can be as expensive as $100 — $200 a call. If you deduct this much from her pay, it would take a lot of toilet scrubbing to pay you back. It is better to limit them if you can.

Answering Your Phone

Non-English speakers have a difficult time answering your phone and taking accurate messages. You probably did not hire your housekeeper to act as your secretary; perhaps an answering machine or a secretary will take better phone messages.

- Teach the people who call you often how to identify themselves in the language of your employee.
- For most day workers, have them ignore your phone.
- Workers who do speak English may be expected to take a few messages but heavy telephone duty interrupts their work.

Visiting With Friends on the Job

In any other industrial job, there would be coffee breaks and times before and after work when friends could get together.

- A worker who lives in your home is entitled to socialization time as well. No one is hired to be on duty 24 hours a day.
- Unless a live-in employee is allowed time to visit with friends in your home (her home too), she is very limited to the amount of time she can socialize.
- Friends alleviate the loneliness of living in your home all week.
- Friends can make a new neighborhood seem less strange and a job more pleasurable.
- Friends of your employee who live or work close by can become your most important source of emergency assistance. A worker who is allowed no time for socialization and consequently knows no one in the neighborhood, can be at a loss in an emergency situation.

Suggestions for Socializing:

- Most live-in housekeepers socialize between the hours of 2 p.m. and 5 p.m. after the bulk of their work is done. You may wish to schedule flexible break and socialization times with your employee.
- She is allowed to visit her friends in their homes of employment, with or without your children. She must ask you whether she may leave and tell you where she will be and when she will return. She may bring your children along only with your consent.
- If any one friend is particularly annoying, you may discuss this person with her. She may agree and need your help to get out of the friendship.

- You don't ever want to call another home for her.
- You prefer not to have her friends intercede for her with you unless language is really a problem.
- She may *never* assign another friend to watch your children while she leaves your home to visit or run an errand, unless there is an emergency situation. For instance, the school calls to have you come for a sick child, you are not home and there is another sick baby at home. She may call someone to stay with the baby while she walks to the school.
- She can visit in her room, in the kitchen or outside, but any congregation is not to disrupt your family.

Night School

If having your employee home every night is crucial to your household, do not hire someone who is going to want to attend night school; young, attractive, and single are obvious clues. If you are already employing this person and the problem has come up or if you agree to allow some evenings off for your employee, try the following:

- Specify the number of nights allowed out, and reasonable times to leave and to return home. Keep this a constant evening or two each week so you can schedule around it.
- Offer daytime instructional activities such as day time classes, tutors, or instructional tapes.

Learning English, any general subjects, or occupational training may be the only way your employee can find better job opportunities. Many housekeepers, especially from other countries, are employed in a home hoping to educate themselves for better opportunities. It may be to your advantage to compromise and to make working and school schedules rather than lose a valued employee to someone who will allow night school.

Night Socializing

- This is a tricky issue. If you can spare her, and won't resent her for leaving, say yes. You need to designate the night each week and the curfew time.
- If dating during the week seems very important to her, you may discuss with her the advantages of day work for women who do need to have more social freedom. Dating can change your role from that of employer to that of a parent for an adolescent. This role does not usually work out for either of you. You may suggest that her husband or special boyfriend visit in the afternoon or evening in your home. We have allowed husbands to sleep over Saturday or Sunday nights when we needed to employ live-in help for a longer period than five days in a row.
- Dating and socializing at night can be very important to your employee. Our strongest recommendation is if you have hired someone to work through Saturday night each week, you establish one or two Saturday nights off for her each month. If a set number of Saturdays would truthfully be impossible for you, do not grant any. The worst and most confusing policy is arbitrarily to give an employee those nights off when you find out that you do not need her. For both of you to organize your social life, these times off need to be constant and established.

Automobile Use

- An employee, especially someone you hire for driving purposes, may wish to use your car for personal reasons also.
- Decide for yourself whether or not automobile use will be permitted for non-work purposes and, if so, under what conditions.
- Many times European "Au Pairs" are hired with the use of the car as a pre-condition of employment.

Keys

Wait until you have passed a trial period of employment. If you aren't home when an employee arrives, keep the key hidden outside in a prearranged spot. After six months employment, you may wish to give your housekeeper her own key.

That "Evening In Paris" Perfume Driving You Crazy?

- Tell her that you or your little boy is highly allergic to perfume and please not to wear it in your home.
- Outline at this time any other dress or personal hygiene procedures you prefer, such as the wearing of sensible, safe shoes, daily bathing, and so forth.

"Gifts?"

- Most employers give presents to their housekeepers for birthdays and for Christmas. Some employers add cash bonuses for these occasions of $30 to $150.
- Used clothing does not count as gifts, nor do gifts count as a replacement for a living wage.

CHAPTER EIGHT

Preparing for Household Help

This chapter outlines the work responsibilities in your home.

This chapter does not include the preparation of a childcare person because childcare is a household responsibility large enough to deserve its own chapters.

Putting Your Own Home in Order

A successful employer must first provide a well organized place of employment. Since this place of employment is your home, you must first organize it and arrange it so that your home represents an efficient work place.

- Remove all useless objects and obstacles, old clothes in closets and hampers, useless knickknacks that don't need dusting and so forth. Don't pay an employee to clean things or move things you don't really need or enjoy.
- Organize each kitchen cabinet and kitchen drawer. Discard broken items and separate seasonal items such as holiday gelatin molds or cookie cutters from every day utensils, gadgets, and kitchenware.
- After all storage areas are appropriately re-arranged and organized, list the contents of each drawer and cabinet and post each list inside the correct place.

If your cleaning person reads in a language other than English, you may wish to translate your lists by using a foreign language dictionary.

- Another easy way to help someone maintain your kitchen, is to take a photograph of each newly straightened drawer and cabinet, encase each photograph in plastic, and place these photos inside each drawer and cabinet.

  Now you will no longer be boiling a sauce, reach for your stirring spoon and grab a carving knife because a cleaning person re-arranged your kitchen.

- Is your cleaning equipment in good working order? Is your vacuum cleaner incapable of blowing a dog's hair let alone picking one up? Is your floor mop dirtier than any floor? If you wash your kitchen floor everytime the dishwasher overflows, it is time to call in the repairman before someone else gets to your home as an employee.

- Do you have sufficient supplies — several cleaning sponges, vacuum cleaner bags, adequate changes of bed linens, and bathroom towels?

- Make sure you have provided sufficient and sensible storage for all your belongings and supplies. Are phonograph records kept in three different places, or children's toys in every room of the house because you have inadequate shelving? Should you keep some changes of children's clothes by the back door because their bedroom is a long walk for anyone? Should you keep bathroom cleaners in the bathroom? Think about how an employee needs to store both your belongings and her cleaning supplies, and try to save steps and headaches.

- Every six months or so check with your employee for her ideas on how to best keep your home well organized and easy to maintain.

"What Cleaning Supplies Should I Provide?"

Ask for any preferences. You will need:

l. Cleaners, liquid cleaner, window cleaner, furniture and floor polishes, toilet bowl cleaners, laundry soaps, and dishwasher needs.

2. Sponges, dust cloths, rags (cut down old towels are good cleaning cloths), sponge mops, dust mops, and brooms.

3. Good quality paper towels are important. All housekeepers dislike cheap paper towels.

4. A bucket and/or carryall to take supplies throughout the house.

5. Any other special cleaning preparation.

6. Rubber gloves.

7. Plastic or paper bags in wastebaskets and some trash collector in every room.

8. A step stool.

Quality cleaning equipment is recommended because all of your supplies are going through more use and need to last longer.

Also, your housekeeper or day cleaners need to inform you of what is in short supply. They can leave you a note or the almost empties.

Professional Supplies

Professional home cleaners purchase only a few cleaning supplies, usually through a janitorial supply house. You too may wish to buy these supplies in bulk at a discount price to cut down on the cost of cleaning supplies, to raise the quality of materials, to have less around for the children to get into, and to make your home a more efficient operation.

From hardware or janitorial supply stores you may wish to purchase:

- A commercial metal bucket on wheels or two buckets if you have an upstairs and downstairs. These are expensive.
- A commercial wet mop with removable mop head.
- A large bottle of concentrated liquid cleaner, usually a disinfectant, used daily in the bathroom or on washable floors. It can eliminate the need for cleansers, scouring soaps, toilet bowl cleaners, marble polish, etc.
- Extra squeeze bottles to mix liquid cleaner and water, one for each bathroom.
- Large commercial dust mop.

Prepare a Schedule

Most housekeepers prefer a daily schedule, not necessarily written out, that outlines a daily routine of jobs to be performed and includes jobs to be accomplished on a weekly basis. In other words, the house and laundry should be cleaned daily but the beds are to be changed on Wednesday, the carpets vacuumed on Thursday, the refrigerator cleaned out on Friday, groceries carried in and put away on Saturday, and so forth. Allow some flexibility.

The following is simply a *sample;* in your home, establish your own priorities. This sample is an approximately 8 1/2 hour day.

7:30 — 8:00 a.m. — The housekeeper is up, showered and dressed, her room is straightened and she is in the kitchen unloading the dishwasher, starting coffee and performing quiet work. Intermediate pay level jobs may include fixing children's breakfast and school lunch.

8:00 — 11:30 a.m. — Bedrooms cleaned, beds made, bathrooms cleaned, furniture dusted, floors swept, breakfast dishes done (as soon after breakfast as possible), kitchen cleaned, and laundry started.

Lunch.

12:30 — 3:00 p.m. — Clothes ironed and put away, extra job for week, floors washed, children watched, played with or walked.

3:00 — 5:30 p.m. — Quiet time, rest.

5:30 — 7:30 p.m. — Table set, help with food preparation, kids' toys straightened, dinner, dinner dishes cleaned, kitchen cleaned, assist children's bath and bed routine.

- For her last work day each week, all jobs should be completed before she leaves. This means there are no dishes left in the dishwasher, clothes in the dryer, or other work left for you to finish.

In A Three-Four Hour Time Frame

A Good Day Cleaner Can:

Reasonably clean
3 rooms

Reasonably clean
1 room and care for
2 children

Sample Daily Schedule for Once a Week Cleaning

Starting time is 8:30 through 9:30.

Morning: Breakfast dishes washed, kitchen cleaned, laundry gathered, load of wash started, bed and bath linens changed, bedrooms straightened, bathrooms washed: sinks, tubs, shower, toilet, floors, mirrors.

Lunch

Afternoon: Living rooms dusted and straightened, dishwasher loaded or unloaded as necessary, kitchen straightened, refrigerator lightly cleaned out, all floors swept, all carpets vacuumed, all trash removed, one load of clean clothes folded and maybe put away.

- Babysitting alters any cleaning schedule. Make allowances in your cleaning expectations if you are also assigning childcare.

- If you hired a day cleaner on a regular basis, you may add one additional half hour job each week from the once a month list such as kitchen cabinets washed out, children's bureau drawer straightened, smudge marks removed from six doors, etc.

- If your home or apartment is small and the work load really only requires a half-day person, consider adding full laundry, plant care, food preparation, or some other duty to both employ this person for a full day's pay and to get more help for yourself. *Only* add these responsibilities if the person you have now is willing to work a full day.

Monthly, Biannual, or Yearly Cleaning Jobs

For some of us the following list is done every decade or if and when we move.

Please, if you have never considered cleaning out your garage or washing your ceiling, do not start now that you have hired help. Some people read this list and instruct their employee to get busy on these jobs right away. Our ceilings are painted, never washed.

Jobs which are starred, or which would not require several days work, can be reasonably included in a housekeeper's list of responsibilities. These jobs are assigned for days when the work load is light or assigned for times when you and your family are away. All others are usually performed by cleaning crews. The entire list can be done by a cleaning crew if your home is gigantic.

1. Window washing — *inside windows or where ladders aren't required.

2. Drapery cleaning and *curtain washing

3. Floor stripping and waxing

* 4. Drawer, closet and cabinet cleanouts

* 5. Wall washing

6. Ceiling washing

7. Carpet shampooing

* 8. Baseboard and woodwork washing

* 9. Hardware such as brass door knobs, hinges, and/or silver polished

*10. Odd room cleanout — attic, garage, cellar — with your help

*11. Odd items cleaned — lamps, light fixtures, pillows, shelves, etc.

TRAINING DO'S AND DON'TS

	DO	DON'T
CLEANING	Apply the correct cleaning product	Use the vacuum to pick up hard or wet objects
LAUNDRY	Separate white clothes from dark clothes	Overload the washer or dryer
IRONING	Use the correct heat temperature	Leave the iron unattended
FOOD STORAGE	Separate refrigerated foods from frozen foods	Put opened jars back in the pantry
COOKING	Use at least one food from each food group each meal:	Overuse salt, sugar or fats
MEAL SERVICE	Set the table each evening like this:	Stack dirty dishes as they are removed from table
DRIVING	Use seat belts and observe all safety laws	Pick up friends or strangers while driving on the job
COMPANION	Ask questions, Share concerns, Report problems	Be afraid of mistakes

CHAPTER NINE

Training Household Help

The job duties and training procedure are arranged in this chapter in an approximate hierarchy of skill level and thus a recommended training order. If you have hired an inexperienced person, you would probably begin teaching cleaning procedures first, move on to laundry instruction, and then demonstrate food storage, purchasing, cooking, driving, and so forth

How to train household help is not only useful information for instructing a new employee, but is also useful information for upgrading the skills and salary of an experienced worker who desires to learn additional responsibilities. Whenever job classifications call for more than beginning wage levels, they are so noted.

"How Do I Begin Training an Inexperienced Person?"

- Our method is to be brief and let her proceed on her own, but we are not fussy or especially good housekeepers. But if you are good and expect the same, you may need to spend a lot of time cleaning right beside her.
- In most cases, if you hired her through a friend of hers, her friends have taken her to their jobs and showed her what is expected.

- For her first full work day, go over your needs with her and teach her each procedure step by step, room by room.
- Assess your priorities. You may need to have prepared a written list for yourself of the cleaning procedures and products for each room. If necessary, a bilingual friend can translate it for you. Employees can use your list as a reminder, but not as a substitute for you; how would you feel if you were handed job lists every day?
- Make your desires clear and reasonable.
- Keep the cleaning solutions simple and show her how to apply them. "Easy Off" on the piano is no fun. It may be necessary to tell your employee to use hot water with cleaning solutions.
- Try to make putting things away, such as jewelry, documents, etc., your responsibility.
- Teach any cleaning principals that you have found helpful over the years, such as sweeping last, soaking rather than scouring stubborn dirt spots, or placing all bed covers flat and tucking in all at once.
- Show her where all belongings are stored in every room and what you want done with questionable items, especially loose paper and mail.
- Teach her how to use your cleaning equipment, appliances, and machinery. Electricity may be a new phenomenon for her. Make sure she understands the dangers of electricity and water, frayed cords, metal in outlets, etc. Clearly demonstrate the proper and improper use of a garbage disposal.
- Teach her how to maintain and care for your equipment, such as emptying the vacuum cleaner bags, cleaning the toaster, removing lint from the dryer. It is helpful to explain why each process is done in a certain manner.

- Teach her any procedures she is to follow if there is a change in weather conditions. Show her which windows to close in case of rain, which drapes to close or open for sunshine, what supplies or clothes to have ready for cold or hot weather.

- Patience will pay off. Don't expect her to have mastered everything in two days. At the end of two to three weeks your home should be running fairly smoothly.

Laundry Training

- Sort your own clothes. Have a separate spot, even if it is a place on the floor, for items that require hand washing or dry cleaning.
- Never assume that your housekeeper knows what is color fast. You read the garment care labels and instruct her.
- Have adequate hampers and at least two baskets or bags to carry clean and dirty clothes.
- If she does not read English, you may want to tape labels in her language on the washer and dryer so that she can understand their control panel settings.
- We recommend that you keep the washing machine set on warm water and keep the dryer set on warm with a time of a half hour. Leave the dials this way for the first month.
- After a while demonstrate how to determine sorting the wash, and how to set water temperature cycles and drying times.
- Supply a small measuring cup for laundry detergent.
- Skip the bleach, fabric softeners and other additives for the first month or so; introduce each one carefully.

- Returning clean clothes to their owners is also difficult. We use the dot system. With a laundry pen, draw one dot in all the clothing of the oldest child. Two dots indicate the second child and so on. Add dots as you pass down the clothes from child to child. So what if your child's teacher thinks that his name is "Two-dot Smith?" At least he will have his own sweater.
- Our children are close in age; to avoid problems of sorting and matching children's socks, we keep all the children's socks in one drawer. First kid to the drawer gets the pair without holes, or simply the only two that match..
- Teach her how to soak clothes and rinse stains immediately. A professional stain removal chart is helpful.
- In time, teach her how to do the hand wash. Supply towels, drying racks, and plastic or wooden hangers.
- Teach her how to iron if you find that she does not know how. Keep the temperature set at medium, buy spray starch and/or a water bottle to make the ironing easier. Explain pressing clothes, ironing on the wrong side, and other ways to avoid burning garments. Show her how to empty water from the iron and how to store it.
- Have a good supply of proper hangers close by and in your closets.

Gretchen:

> *"The worst thing that happened to me was the time at my first job that I picked up all my boss's shirts and ties and suits that were lying in a pile. I put them all in the washing machine and was ready to put them in the dryer when the employer walked in. I think she screamed and almost fainted. She told me I should have asked, but added that I probably didn't know any better because my father had only one pair of pants. This wasn't true. My father wore suits to work, but it was never my job to wash them. I felt just terrible."*

Food Storage

- In many countries of the world food is bought fresh daily and cooked each day. We in the U.S. tend to buy food less frequently and have adequate storage and refrigeration. The food and refrigeration process may be completely foreign to an inexperienced housekeeper.

- Go over your pantry, vegetable bin, refrigerator and freezer. Make sure your food storage makes sense.

- To avoid having cat food with the tuna, try to buy the same brands for the first weeks. Your employee can recognize the color of the can and put it with others.

- Explain the uses of foil, plastic wrap, Tupperware, or whatever you use to store food.

- Show her how to peel the carrots, wash lettuce, slice celery and cucumbers or any other fresh vegetable and put these in lock type plastic bags. Some vegetables are best stored unwashed. Explain this to your employee.

- Explain which jars, when opened, go in the refrigerator. Opened mayonnaise can begin to smell quite unpleasant when left on the shelf.

- Have her ask you where to put any uncertain item. If you cannot be around, tell her to please store the item in the refrigerator.

- Be patient; a rage over a $.79 package of refrigerated rolls found in the pantry is not worth it.

- When she unloads the bags from the grocery store, she needs to be told what is frozen and what is not. It is no fun to find the roast you intended for dinner frozen solid at 6 p.m.

Grocery Shopping

- It is advisable that you show a new housekeeper how to grocery shop even if marketing is not to be her responsibility. One grocery trip is recommended for two reasons. First, your employee may want certain items for herself and may wish to purchase these items and to familiarize herself with the products carried by your local market. The other reason to take an employee to the store is that if you are unable to get there yourself, your employee knows where the market is, knows what to buy, and can shop for you even if someone else must drive her there.
- Grocery shopping by an employee on a regular basis is an added skill and needs to be paid for at a higher than starting salary level.
- To train a person you have hired to grocery shop, first review your food supplies with this person. Explain how much of each item you keep on hand and when you consider it time to replace or replenish each item.
- Outline an approximate meal plan for the week utilizing family preferences, good nutrition, and the food section of the newspaper to take advantage of seasonal products.
- Read the food section together to determine other store specials or savings ideas.
- Make out a shopping list utilizing your needs, menu plan and store specials. Make out the list of items in the order that they are found in the store.
- Go to the market together.
- Teach unit buying, explaining how to read the shelf markings. Are 16 oz. of tomatoes a better per ounce price than a 4 oz. can? Which is the best buy — the jumbo, giant, or two queen size packages of detergent? Don't be afraid of bulk buying just because you could never carry that large box of detergent or disposible diapers into the house; your employee may be able to.

- Teach her how to read the label for ingredients and specify which additives, preservatives, salts or sweeteners you wish to include or eliminate.
- Place items in the cart in a sensible order such as canned goods first, frozen and perishable foods last. Keep soaps separated from foods they could flavor.
- Determine how your employee will pay for the marketing and whether or not you need to make check payment arrangements with the store management.
- Make out the next week's list with her as you go along and let her proceed on her own.

Training To Cook

Unless you are paying extra for cooking, her cooking duties at a starting level salary may include vegetable and fruit salad preparation, the children's breakfast and lunch, and preparing the children's dinner when you are not home. You may want to see what her own cooking repertoire is.

To train her to do these meals and preparation and eventually to take on more cooking responsibilities:

- Purchase a beginning or basic cookbook that explains, and hopefully illustrates, cooking basics; check off what she does or doesn't know how to do.
- Teach her to clean, peel, and slice vegetables as they come from the grocery store, combining them to become the salad that she can assemble whenever you choose.
- Mentally return to junior high school cooking class. Teach her the basic four food groups and begin with breakfast preparation: milk and dairy products, cereals and breads, fruits and vegetables, meats and eggs.
- Make sure you are instructing her on cooking safety, such as proper flame level, use of pot holders and sharp knives.

- Stressing the basic four food groups again, teach her to make the children's or your lunch: salads, fruit, meat, vegetables, sandwiches, soups, etc.
- Children's dinners can be the same as lunches with the addition of spaghetti, chicken, hamburgers, cooked vegetables, and cooked starches.
- An easy family dinner can now be added. Teach her to put some of those vegetables in a crock pot or stew pot and add meat. Use the same procedure for adding rice or another starch. If she cannot read English, buy the same few brands and help her memorize the package directions.
- You may buy bottled sauces, prepared bread crumbs, grated cheeses, or canned soups to put over meats, fish, or for vegetable casseroles.
- Work with her to plan simple menus. Teach color and texture balance. Buy her the ingredients and let her try.
- An experienced housekeeper may teach you, but if you follow these steps with a person who could not cook before, you should succeed in teaching an employee how to cook.

Meal Service

- Table setting can be learned by an inexperienced housekeeper by showing her a table setting diagram found in most cookbooks, adding your own preferences, and setting the table with her for the first time.
- Food service beyond table setting needs to be compensated for at a higher than beginning level salary.
- Outline linens, dishes, tableware to be used for each meal, including serving platters and serving utensils, trivets or hot plates, flowers and decor.
- Determine how you wish meals served — do you prefer all food brought to the table in serving plates or do you prefer individual service in which a portion of each food is placed on individual plates in the kitchen and brought to each person? Some prefer a combination: some dishes brought to the table on platters while the main part of the meal is placed on each plate in the kitchen. Others prefer that the main course is set before the host who serves the first portion. The employee stands to the left of the host, removes the filled plate from the host and gives the host an empty plate while handing the full plate to the first person to be served.
- Platters are removed with the right hand and plates placed for the next course with the left hand where formal service is required.
- Clearing away the main course should be done by removing the food plates first then the serving platters and then the unused dishes. Avoid piling dishes. Brush away crumbs.
- Coffee and dessert are usually served on a completely cleared table.

Training a Companion for the Elderly or the Handicapped

Many sections of this book provide information and ideas about the employment of a companion. For example, the guidelines presented in the childcare chapters apply to the employment of all companions for anyone — an invalid, an aging relative, or a handicapped dependent.

- If you are hiring a companion for a home other than your own and will not be supervising the work on a daily basis, we advise you to hire an English speaking person with housekeeping or companion experience.
- Explain the special needs, abilities, and limitations of the person for whom you are hiring a companion.
- Teach the companion any special procedures followed in the work home such as how beds are to be made, special diet information, special pet care, exercise information, and so forth.
- If the companion does not drive, you can teach this person how to shop for groceries, clothing or other goods by bus, taxi, or telephone. Provide her with a list of delivery services.
- One of her main functions is to be available in the case of an emergency. Make certain that she can summon help (knows how to let police, ambulance, and fire companies enter security buildings such as condominiums) and is familiar with all the information in the emergency section of this book.
- While training this person to work comfortably and capably in the home, decide which decisions are yours to make, which belong to the person living in the home, and which are to be made by the home companion. Communicate this information clearly.

Driving

- If you are hiring a person to drive who already has a valid drivers' license, the following additional training is recommended.
- Check the validity of the drivers' license and the driving record through your local police department or Department of Motor Vehicles.
- Take several test rides, choosing sites that have various road and driving conditions such as a freeway, a neighborhood street, and a congested area.
- Go over any particular driving procedures that you want followed, including special caution areas in your neighborhood.
- Driver and passengers must wear seat belts. Small children must be in safety seats.
- If the driver will be using your car, go over all car features with this person. Make sure he or she can operate headlights, radio, windshield wipers, etc. without taking his or her eyes off the road.
- Whether the driver will use your car or their own, oversee the maintenance and mechanical condition of the car they use for you.
- Check your insurance coverage to make sure all vehicles, all drivers, property, and passengers are covered.
- Make sure registration is current.
- If your driver will be participating in car pools or driving other people, advise the other people that you have hired a driver. Introduce them to the driver and take your driver through the car pool route so they are familiar with the people and places.
- Check from time to time with the people in the car pool as to the performance of the driver.

Training a Non-Driver to Drive

- Training a non-driver to drive can be a long and nerve wracking process. (Remember when you were 16?) You are more than welcome to go over a handbook on how to drive and to take a person to an empty lot or roadway and begin teaching behind the wheel driving.
- You may desire instead to hire a driving teacher or driving school to teach your employee how to drive and how to pass your state's driving exam.
- In either case, once your employee has obtained a valid drivers license, you may increase his or her job responsibilities to include driving for you and increase their salary accordingly.

Hire a Consultant

If you really don't want to be involved in training of some specific field of housework or home maintenance, hire a consultant.

For example, if you want an employee to take over plant care in your home but know nothing about plants except how to kill them slowly, call a plant care company who is willing to send someone to teach you and/or your employee the names of the plants, what they like to eat, and when to water. It costs about $10 for a half hour consultation.

- You can do the same for efficient care of any portion of the housework. For a cooking consultant, call cooking schools or high schools or colleges who employ cooking teachers; for an entertaining consultant, find a caterer; for a cleaning consultant, call a cleaning contractor. Many firms advertise in apartment owners manuals and in the yellow pages.

- Finally, someone else's housekeeper may be just the person to hire for teaching new or better skills to your employee. Pay an experienced worker for one hour to one week for training.

Training — If You're Never Home

- If you will rarely or never be at home while a household employee works, hire her for her first time for an evening or weekend to introduce her to you, your home, and your needs. Pay her for this introductory time.
- Again, consider hiring another experienced worker to train your new employee. Pay the experienced worker a higher wage and your new worker less for this one to two day training period.
- You may leave clear instructions by notes or tape recorder or through a phone call. If the employee doesn't speak English, have someone with you who speaks her language or can make the tapes or telephone calls. But it is helpful and advisable to have some personal communication between the two of you.
- Recall an interpretor after about 2 — 6 months of employment to make sure you are communicating all praise and problems.

Who Does What List

	Name	Phone
Plumber		
Electrician		
Electric Company		
Exterminator		
Gas Company		
Delivery Dry Cleaning		
Telephone Company		
Delivery Pharmacy		
Handiman		
Rug Cleaner		
Roofer		
Pet Groomer		
Veterinarian		
Yard Cleaner—Gardener		
Dentist		
Hairdresser		
Fast Food Delivery		
Department Stores		

Add authorized expenditures, credit card numbers, account numbers, contact people, etc.

CHAPTER TEN

Introducing a Childcare Person to Your Household

Because childcare is said to be the number one challenge facing the American woman in the eighties, how to successfully employ competent care for your child in your own home becomes the most significant portion of this book

Whether you have employed or are about to employ a housekeeper, babysitter, nanny, governess, or the teenager next door, the guidelines presented in this chapter will help you. We will use the word "housekeeper" to describe the childcare person, although "housekeeper" does not do justice to the person who, with your training and guidance, will assist you in the raising of your children.

"Who's She, Mommy?" How to Introduce Help to Your Child

- Explain to your child why you have hired childcare help. For example, say the housekeeper is here to help you around the house, or so that you can go to school or to work. Use this opportunity to point out to your child that successful people get help.
- Outline the job duties of this new employee and explain how these responsibilities will affect your child. Someone new may be staying with him in the afternoons and doing the wash, but he still must continue to clear the table, and you will continue to cook dinner.

- Answer all fears and concerns your child may have about being left in the care of another. Share his concerns with your housekeeper and encourage him to talk about these anxieties as long as seems reasonable.

- Help your child and your housekeeper get to know each other. You can do this by encouraging dialogue between them. Help your child learn to ask questions and to learn about her background, language, and customs. Help your housekeeper ask your child for information and conversation.

- Assure your child that you are his parent, and you will always be his parent.

What Is Your Role?

- You and your husband are the real parents. No one can take this primary relationship and responsibility from you.

- Your role is to train and guide your assistant so that he or she can best provide for the well being of your child.

- Your role is to make this person's transition into your home easier for yourself, your child, and your employee. See Chapter Thirteen for information on how to be a successful manager.

- Your role is to relinquish some power and some control. Enjoy your housekeeper's relationship with your child.

- The most effective way for you, for your employee, and for your child to view the role of your childcare person is as your partner or as your assistant. This person is an employee, not a slave, not your twin, not another child, and not a permanent member of your family.
- Your role is to communicate a partnership relationship clearly, carefully, and as often as necessary to yourself, your employee, your spouse and your child. You are all in this together.

The Role of Your Childcare Person

- Your childcare person is your partner. She and you share the same goal of excellent care for your children. As a paid assistant, she is to help you and to follow the guidelines and philosophy you have established.
- Her role is to insure the safety and well being of your child and to emotionally support your child with acceptance and affection.
- Your childcare person has her own style; you need to accept some of her views and methods if they are not harmful for your child.
- Her role is never inferior. You cannot be partners with a person whose background or culture you judge to be inferior.

Marta Ruiz:

> *"I never think of my employer's children as my own. They are the children of my boss. I take good care of them and I care for them a lot, but I am relieved of the responsibility of buying their needs, educating them, or wondering how they will turn out. These concerns I keep for my own children."*

Role of Your Child

- To be a child — not the employer of the housekeeper, not the "real person" left in charge.
- To learn how to relate to other adult figures in his life.
- To respect and carry out directives from the housekeeper.
- To continue to share in the household responsibilities.
- To be a good friend to your housekeeper — respectful of her privacy, interested in her as a person, and aware of her separate life.

Where Everything is Kept

A childcare person needs to know the whereabouts of many household items and children's belongings in your home. Explain where you keep the following:

- Children's clothes, toys, mealtime, bedding, and diapering needs
- Clean-up equipment, paper towels, brooms, cleaners, etc.
- Light bulbs
- Tweezers
- Television, radio, video recorders, and their operating directions
- First aid kit
- Paper and pencils
- Scissors and sewing supplies
- Candles and flashlights
- Pet supplies — leashes, food
- Medicines if directed to administer
- Keys — spare house keys and car keys if necessary

- Plunger

- And we keep and use often (for rocks down sinks, dolls stuck in jars, and uses our children have yet to create) — surgical tongs

- Appliance operating instructions

- Quirks and crazies of your home

- "Don't touches" — security system, computer, appliances, and so forth.

Working Together

Sharon Brandon discusses how she has formed a partnership:

> *"I have tried to impress upon my children that a magic wand is not waved over the house everyday while they are at school and, presto, the house is immaculate, but that real work is involved. So that's why my children are assigned chores and are encouraged to do them. They keep their rooms neat, make their beds, carry their clean clothes from Rosario's room to their own, and feed the animals. Rosario knows the children care about her and that they care about her work. Their concern forms a loving relationship.*
>
> *My children can't give orders to the housekeeper. My children would never refer to a housekeeper, anyone's housekeeper, as a maid. I know that some of their friends do, but not around here. One teenage boy patted Rosario on the bottom. When I questioned his behavior, he said that it was 'okay, because she was just a maid'. After he apologized, he was quickly shown to the door. Treating the housekeeper with respect has not been much of a problem because our children have always gotten along well with our housekeepers — it is my job to teach them how."*

CHAPTER ELEVEN

Training a Childcare Person

Childcare may not be natural for anyone. A good job in your home begins with proper training. Unlike most babysitting situations, a live-in housekeeper has the advantage of observing your methods and procedures before she cares for your child on her own. Make good use of this observation time together.

Babies

- List for yourself her responsibilities with the baby. Walk her through your schedule, demonstrating responsibilities such as how you want a diaper put on, what you want the baby to wear, when you want him to nap, when you want him awakened from his nap, and when you want him fed.
- Read with her the Appendix section on Emergencies and Safety and go over these procedures emphasizing those most important to you and adding any of your own you deem necessary. Be clear and firm.
- Stress again that the baby is your *first* priority. Any problems that she may have with the baby are to be reported to you immediately.

- Your baby's housekeeping needs and laundry requirements are often different from those your housekeeper does for the rest of the family. Therefore, you may want your housekeeper to know how to sterilize a bottle, pacifier, and other equipment; wash the baby's clothes, including the use of special soaps, double rinsing, and stain treatments; store and care for the baby's clothes and toys; to avoid dangerous foods, toys, pets, and household hazards; to secure the baby on the changing table, the infant seat, and the stroller; and to refrigerate unused formula and food.
- If your childcare person does not speak English, make certain that you have communicated your needs clearly — either by using a dictionary, demonstrating with a doll, or by going through these special responsibilities with a translator. Use any way you can think of to communicate why you want certain procedures followed.

Additional Duties With All Children

Mothers who are assigning childcare to the housekeeper on a more sporadic basis usually outline the housekeeper's duties as they go along and do not use a list. The instructions for a housekeeper in either case should include:

- **Nutrition** — Outline what food you want prepared for your children. Too much junk food snacking can be a problem for mothers and housekeepers alike. Some child guidance professionals suggest a snack drawer that the children can help themselves to. Sometimes you can give the housekeeper a snack container. Establish your own nutritional preferences and communicate them to your housekeeper.

- **Safety** — Stress to her that she is in charge. You remove unsafe articles from the home and go over with her the safety portion of this book.

- **Recreation** — Decide whether or not you are paying for a friend for your child. If you do wish the housekeeper to initiate or participate in your child's play, we have listed numerous suggestions starting on page 128.

- **Toy maintenance** — Have ample storage space for blocks, puzzles, little people, etc., and have the children help her with putting toys away properly. This is a difficult area for many housekeepers. You and your child may have to help her understand what is trash and what is a "treasure". You may wish to have her place all questionable items in one box which you and your child can periodically reevaluate.

- **Clothing** — Teach her proper clothing for school, play, and dress up occasions. Make certain that all are weather and color appropriate also. Children's clothes may require immediate washings to remove stains or to keep one item continuously clean, such as a blanket or favorite shirt.

- **Whereabouts and socializing** — A housekeeper can be assigned the responsibility for knowing and/or approving your child's whereabouts. Show your housekeeper who lives where and at what school or play yard different activities occur. Inform your children to check all plans with the housekeeper first. You may wish to make out a chart of everyone's comings and goings, children's friends, and phone numbers. Decide with her which friends are allowed over and which parents may pick up and/or return your children.

Suggested Activities for Your Child and Your Housekeeper

A housekeeper doesn't necessarily sweep the floor with one arm and teach ballet with the other, but she can become involved in certain activities which will offer an alternative to the old standby, "You kids watch television while I iron."

Remember: She may not finish ironing.

- If your childcare person was hired solely for childcare, these suggested activities are part of the job description.

Play

- Have your housekeeper take walks with your child. They can go around the block, through parks, etc. To add interest, suggest the following:

  - Collection walks. Find bottle caps, flowers, leaves, etc.

  - Listening walks. Listen for animal sounds, traffic sounds, etc.

  - Foreign language walks. Learn the names of trees, flowers, etc.

  - Collage walks. Collect objects to bring home and glue on paper. Label paper bags for each child and have him collect all items that match the label, such as "something soft", "green things", etc.

- Your housekeeper and child can do imitation housework together, such as doll or toy washing, sweeping, soap suds play. Have sponges and buckets for your child and observe safety rules.

- Your child may do art work with your housekeeper. Have supplies for painting, coloring, pasting, office supplies, clay modeling, etc.

- Your housekeeper may be a good seamstress, so take advantage of her skills and suggest that she work with your child. They can begin with sewing cards or stitching material strips. They can advance to making doll clothes, doing embroidery, crocheting, knitting, spool weaving, or sewing buttons. Some housekeepers have designed and made with children wonderful costumes with capes, hats, old curtains, gowns, etc. With supervision, they can then dye their material creations in food colors, coffee, beet juice, or tea solutions or practice tie dyeing.
- Your housekeeper may invite another housekeeper and small child over for play groups. Or she may visit the home of a neighbor so that your child can play with others.

Kitchen Crafts

Your housekeeper need not know how to cook in order to participate in the following "cooking" activities with your child.

- They can make salads: vegetables, fruit, tuna, egg, or jello.
- We use unflavored gelatin, fruit juice, and canned, fresh, or frozen fruit because it involves more mixing. Follow package directions and teach your housekeeper how to measure, use heat-proof measuring cups and bowls. Teach her how to handle boiling water.
- They can mix yogurt and juice and freeze as popsicles.
- They can make things from bread, cookie, tortilla, pie, or pasta dough.
- Consult a children's cookbook for hundreds of cooking and non-cooking activities to do in the kitchen.

Games and Quasi-Learning Activities for Non-English Speakers

- If your childcare person does not speak English, there are foreign language coloring books, story books, and read-along tapes available in foreign language book stores. If you know of someone traveling to your housekeeper's native country, give her some money to bring back some of these materials for your employee. Or, ask your housekeeper to have some children's books mailed to you both. Or call your library.
- "Sesame Street Magazine" has a complete activity explanation page written in Spanish. If your housekeeper can read in Spanish, she can help your child with the magazine's activities.
- You can make your own tapes to occupy your child while you are away from home. They can range from reading activities and workbook instructions to piano lesson practices.
- Your housekeeper can sit in on a card or board game, jigsaw puzzle, video game and so forth.

Activities Not Allowed

Don't be shy here. If any activities look remotely dangerous to you, say so and put it on your "not allowed" list. This is ours:

- Any unsupervised cooking, baking, frying or toasting
- Using sharp scissors or knives
- Shrinky dinks
- Glitter in the house
- Super type glue
- Ironing — or any electrical appliance "games"
- Games with small pieces or sewing near the baby

- Dress up with long costumes
- Playing with bikes in the street
- Swimming
- Playing golf, hardball, and other rough games
- Continuous television viewing or video game playing

Keep This in Mind: If You Want a Playground Director, Hire One

- Some housekeepers enjoy playing with children very much. Others do not. Discuss her preferences before you suggest activities. If your child does well at initiating his own play, your housekeeper needs only to check upon the safety of his games.
- Clean-ups need to be a joint effort, with the child taking on the larger amount of responsibility.
- You need to calculate the hours your housekeeper must spend with your child in these play activities as a part of her hourly wage rate. Playing does not count as her "rest period" even though it looks like she is having fun.
- Supervising, initiating, or participating in your child's play can improve the relationship between your housekeeper and your child. With your guidance, your home can become an enriching environment for them both.

Childcare Training Classes

- To further facilitate the training of a childcare person, some employers have taken childcare classes with their employee.
- You may find neighborhood classes in nutrition, first aid, self-esteem, and so forth helpful for you both.

CHAPTER TWELVE

The Most Common Childcare Issues and What to Do About Them

Parents have expressed a variety of concerns and questions about hiring household help to care for their children. This chapter will discuss the concerns we heard most often. Safety was a large enough issue to be covered more thoroughly in a section of its own. See the Appendix for a discussion of emergency and safety precautions. Language concerns are discussed primarily in Chapter Two.

Jealousy

Sometimes a mother is jealous or resentful of having to share her baby with someone else. The mother may need to feel indispensable yet at the same time need to be relieved of some of the constant demands on her time by a new born baby. When the baby seems very content in the arms of another, some mothers become confused and jealous of this unforeseen relationship.

- Remember that a housekeeper must form a relationship with your baby if she is to become a competent caretaker. Understand, too, that she may miss her own children and family very much and your baby is someone whom she can love and from whom she can receive love.

- Trust that her affection for your child could be very emotionally healthy for your baby in that your baby is loved by another adult.
- Try to control your jealousy by redefining the relationship. Some mothers fantasize that the housekeeper is the child's favorite aunt. Other mothers refer to their infant as "our" baby, meaning the baby is the mother's and the housekeeper's.
- Avoid assigning the total care of your infant to the housekeeper. Save more responsibility than the 2 a.m. feeding for yourself. Some mothers who do not honestly enjoy the care of a newborn turn over the baby's entire care to a housekeeper and then reclaim their baby when he is at an age that they feel more comfortable dealing with. Reclaiming your baby after a year or so my be emotionally difficult for all three of you — baby, the housekeeper, and you.
- Tell your housekeeper that you are experiencing feelings of jealousy concerning her relationship with the baby. Explain to her that you want the baby to spend more time with you and you want more control over the care of the baby. If you cannot regain an appropriate relationship with your own child because your childcare person is overbearing, you may have to terminate this employment.

Improper Feeding

Your childcare person may be giving your baby or small child a bottle or food at his slightest whimpering. She may be overfeeding the baby, or feeding the baby inappropriate food such as sugar water or finger food that he could choke on. She could be feeding your child food you find inappropriate — but be a little liberal here. One housekeeper was fired for giving the child a tortilla which, although "foreign", is perfectly healthy. It is more important to remember that food is often a gift of love and affection.

- Improper feeding may occur because the housekeeper believes that a well-fed baby is a happy one. Also, she may believe that the baby has food preferences which she likes to satisfy. In either case, she does not like to hear your baby cry and will do what she can to pacify a crying child.

- Suggest other activities that she can do with a crying baby such as walking him, singing to him or playing music, rocking him or letting him cry for five minutes before he is fed.

- Inform your housekeeper that the doctor does not want the baby fed so often because it is bad for his weight or for his heart. Sometimes citing an authority figure such as the doctor works well.

- Check your priorities again. If your housekeeper believes that a clean home is your most important need, then feeding the baby anything at anytime may be the only way she knows to keep him quiet long enough for her to finish scrubbing the bathroom.

Discipline

- To make her job easier, remove from her control all inappropriate toys and objects. Lock the pool gate and store inappropriate clothes. Eliminate potential arguments that your child may have with the housekeeper over what he may or may not play with by having the "may nots" out of sight.

- Talk with her and state your needs. Make sure she knows why you want your child controlled in a certain manner. Get her feedback on her greatest areas of difficulty with your child.

- Suggest that she use positive reinforcement when the child performs appropriately such as "I like the way you put your toys away."

- Encourage her to be in control. "No" is a good word and you want her to use it with your child. You will not be upset if he cries because she told him no. She is not to allow a child of any age to be her employer.

- If you ever suspect that she utilizes "Boogie Man" stories, superstitions, or religious teachings that are greatly divergent from your beliefs, put a stop to this method of control.

- Determine whether you have allowed her to form a loving relationship with your child. If she cares about him, she will understand the need to set limits. If she has no concern for him or you, she is not capable of working with children. If, however, she is rarely left with the children, she may not have been given the time to relate well with them.

- Talk with your child. It is time for him to begin internalizing your standards of behavior. The child must know that you set the limits for his behavior even when you are not home. Tell your child that he will be restricted for infractions of your rules or for disobeying the housekeeper. If bedtimes, for example, are out of control, call in at nine. When a small voice answers, ground him.

- Leave some room for your housekeeper's style of discipline. She cannot be a carbon copy of you. Nor can she be expected to be stern with the child in those areas of behavior which you cannot control. Compliment her when you both are doing better at setting and maintaining limits.

Sharon Brandon:

> *"It can be frightening for a child to have too much control or power. So many housekeepers are afraid of the children because the employers have not defined their roles so that the housekeeper thinks that the kids are her boss too. The housekeeper needs to be told that rude behavior is unacceptable. I say things like, 'You are the adult, you are the boss when I am not here.' I am the type of mother who is always right there for her children, ready to show them that I love them and support them. As a result, my children come to expect quite a bit from me. They expect me to jump when they call. Although I am 'on duty' with my kids when I am home, if I run out of steam, the housekeeper is always willing and available to satisfy my kids' needs. While it is good for children to get all this love, I don't believe that it is a good thing for children to have every demand met. They rarely feel frustrated and they rarely appreciate the amount of work that it takes to satisfy their demands. I have had to set limits with myself, with Rosario, and with the children."*

Remaining the "Real Parent"

Most parents have no trouble remaining the primary nurturer or the "real parent" to their child. For those parents who fear that the presence of capable childcare people will make them lose loving contact with their child, we offer the following:

- Maintain daily contact with your child. If you are gone all day at work, establish a phone-in time for your child so that he can call you and have some uninterrupted time with you. This special phone-in time will allow your child to express his concerns to you.
- Devise as many ways you can think of to know approximately what goes on at home when you are not there. Ask questions, stop home occasionally, ask a neighbor or relative to visit. Let the children know that you are interested in what goes on at home, even when you cannot always be there.
- Stay in close contact with your child's teachers and coaches.
- Attend as many school functions or activities as possible. If you have Columbus Day off from work and the schools are open, arrange with the teacher to do volunteer classroom work on that day. Attend a few after school practices even if someone else drives the carpool. Not only do children interpret your attendance as showing an interest in what they do, but you will gain good information about the people who work with your child and how your child relates to his surroundings. (For special performances, invite your childcare people. After all, they have all helped get your child to practice or had his uniform clean and ready).
- Do not allow an employee to be overly critical of your style of parenting. Her suggestions are helpful, but too much criticism undermines your role.

- Keep involved with your community, a task difficult for many full time working mothers, but often well worth the effort. Your community can help you find playmates for your child, friends for yourself, help for your childcare person, a source of babysitters and back-up assistance, and another way to know what is going on in your child's life.

- Explain to your child that your physical presence is not the only way a parent demonstrates love for a child. Your child is with you in your thoughts even when you are not with him. Communicate how he is a part of your life.

Dan Stern:

"My mother hired a nurse to care for me when I was born and she stayed until I was two years old. No one remembers her name and it is very strange for me to think that someone fed me and probably saw my first step and heard my first word, and I don't even know who she is.

After the nurse left, a woman named Leona came to work for us. She was the mainstay of my life in terms of actual care, physically and emotionally. She stayed with us for seven years. I loved Leona, but as I got older I began to fantasize what it might be like to have a parent who was actually interested in what I thought or did. I remember Leona taking me to Little League practice or to the dentist and I'd be wishing it were my father or mother. I used to hold class offices and my parents would never even know about it.

Leona was like a mother to me because she took care of me and she cared for me as a person. But I was in a real conflict about my feelings for her because I knew that her place in the household was subordinate to my parents and inferior to them in the most negative sense of the word. The message was that I, too, was superior to Leona. Yet she was the person whom I loved, needed, and admired.

When Leona left when I was nine years old, I was not at all prepared for her departure. No one told me that she was leaving our home. It is difficult to express how I felt the day she left. It was a heart wrenching experience that I remember with more pain than I felt for my parents' divorce. Really, I don't remember my father leaving for the last time, but I will never forget seeing Leona driving off.

As a parent, I can now understand that my mother was not capable of being an effective parent. She was not a happy person. She would have found a way to avoid parenting without household help. She did not enjoy raising children. I think it was okay that she hired someone to give us the emotional care that she didn't feel capable of giving. But, if she had been a little more visible, a little more interested, and a little more caring, and if she had treated the people she hired as equal partners and good people, I would have received a much clearer message as to what was going on and been able to understand that more than one person could love and "mother" me.

Obviously, I have strong ideas about the kind of relationship that develops between my children and people who live and work in our home. I have made it clear that working in someone's home is a job; no greater, no less, than any other job. We show our children where each household worker lives to help them make contact with their personal life. Our kids know that Marta works in our house for money and because she enjoys her work, but she has her own home in another community. They have met her family. We have taken the mystery out of who the housekeeper is, where she really lives, and why she is working for us. There is nothing degrading about knowing Marta and her family and understanding the economics of the entire situation, hers and ours.

There is no reason for household help to prevent a person from parenting his own children. I do not use Marta as a way to abandon my parental role and neither does June. Marta is respected and admired and vice versa. Her affection is good for our kids, but should she leave tomorrow, our children would miss her but would survive.

When the Housekeeper Leaves Your Job

The termination of your housekeeper's or babysitter's employment may have an undesirable effect on your child. Miguel Ramirez, a child guidance specialist in Los Angeles, often interviews housekeepers and babysitters along with the parents and siblings of children he sees in his practice. Mr. Ramirez believes that a child may view the disappearance of the housekeeper as a loss similar to that suffered in a death or divorce. He may blame himself for this loss. It is therefore unwise to ever tell a child that if he doesn't listen to the housekeeper, she will leave or you will fire her. He then feels the housekeeper left because he was bad.

- He may feel relieved that the housekeeper is gone. If the family's relationship with the housekeeper was particularly stormy, a child of three or older may be very aware of the problems and be glad that the source of friction is gone.

- He may become angry and act out his anger or hold back his feelings and seem despondent when the housekeeper leaves. He may be angry with you. Ramirez suggests that you help him verbalize his feelings. Those same feelings may make it difficult for him to adjust to a new housekeeper. He may not wish to risk another emotional involvement. Give him time to adjust to his loss and to the new person.

To Make a Housekeeper's or Childcare Person's Leaving Easier on Your Child

Spend as much time with your child as possible. Even if you are away all day, schedule time for your child. If free time and quality time are coming from you, the parent, your child will not be in a state of shock when a childcare person leaves.

- Do hire different babysitters from time to time. An advantage of other babysitters is that your child learns different people can care for him in your absence. Using other babysitters helps to break the adult triad — you, your husband, and the housekeeper — that he could become used to.
- Take advantage of any opportunity to explain your housekeeper's work situation. If your child wonders where the housekeeper is on her day off, explain that she works for you Tuesdays through Saturdays but today she is with her friends. Point out that someday she may no longer work at your home. Tell him that she will still care for him and think about him when she no longer works for you. A child who truly understands the private life and work situation of the housekeeper may feel a sense of loss but also will understand the need for economic or personal advancement. Therefore, he can accept the departure of the housekeeper better than you imagined.

- If and when the parting of the ways does come, it helps to keep it amicable enough so that the housekeeper can visit your child and gradually taper off their relationship. Phase out a former housekeeper by retaining her on Mondays even though she may be 9 1/2 months pregnant and cannot really do housework. She can use the money and your child will appreciate the contact.

- If your housekeeper leaves without warning, simply tell your child the truth. Say that she was no longer happy in your home for reasons that had nothing to do with him. She needed to find a better paying job, a job that allowed her to be with her boyfriend, or she was ready to move elsewhere. Discuss these eventual possibilities from time to time.

- Keep photographs of your child with the various housekeepers. You will have pictures for your child of all the people who have helped care for him. Give a copy to the housekeeper. Some housekeepers receive photographs in the mail every year of former employers' children.

- Sometimes a housekeeper will discuss with the child why she intends to leave. You may or may not be privy to their discussion. But if she does talk to the child, he may not be at all surprised to see that she is gone.

Leaving the Children With the Housekeeper When You Go Away

- If you have had your housekeeper for a good period of time and her relationship with your children is caring and trustworthy, then you may definitely leave her in charge, especially for short trips.
- The housekeeper knows their routine, their special needs, their friends. You may wish to hire someone to help her, such as a neighborhood babysitter who will walk or play with one or more of your children.
- You may prepare daily surprise bags that contain a small toy game or activity and/or some kind of special food. Leave all bags with the housekeeper to be given out each day and add additional activities for her to hand out when she finds it necessary.
- Leave your itinerary with all necessary phone numbers, including area codes.
- Prepare a written schedule of each child's daily activities.
- Go over the charts in advance with each child and your childcare person. Include phone numbers of everyone involved (example: carpool drivers, coaches, religious schools, homes your children will visit, etc.).
- Go over the Emergency Section of this book. Decide who needs to be contacted and what needs to be done in an emergency situation when you cannot be reached. Contact the people who will assist your childcare person in an emergency and advise them of your departure and arrival dates, your itinerary and any other important information (including phone numbers) about your children, pets or household.
- In the unlikely event that your childcare person must leave your home for short or long periods of time, line up back up baby sitters.

- Leave the phone numbers of all necesary household repair services, and delivery services such as markets, take out food establishments and pharmacies.
- Make certain that there is ample cash for food, entertainment, special treats and/or emergencies.

"Can I Take the Housekeeper With Us on Vacation?"

You may, but consider the following suggestions:

- Buy any extra clothes that she may need such as a bathing suit or a ski parka.
- Give her a separate vacation time with pay.
- If her visa papers are not in order, be careful crossing agricultural and country border checkpoints.
- Pay her at a higher rate if she works on her usual day off.

"What Do I Do if I Suspect Child Abuse?"

- Observe the housekeeper or babysitter with your child.
- Investigate any complaints by your child, any fears of being left alone, or any refusal on his part to be touched by the housekeeper.
- Don't ignore any suspicions of child abuse — to do so would be to act as an accomplice.
- Confront your employee immediately.

CHAPTER THIRTEEN

Promoting Good Work Performance

Learning to be a good manager and to promote satisfying work performance is not easy. You as the employer may for the first time ever find yourself totally responsible for the working conditions, pay scale, training, and supervision of an employee. Working in your home may also be your employee's first job.

In addition to your lack of experience as a manager, work in the home is not entirely analogous to work outside the home. How many factory workers would know the intimate details of his manager's personal life the way a home employee has access to such personal information? Intimacy can erase the normal employer/ employee distance; management can be more difficult.

Unlike industry, the home produces no specific or consistent product. The work is often confusing and difficult. A factory seamstress does not witness her product being ripped to shreds the way a housekeeper often watches a just cleaned room destroyed in three minutes by two children. Children, telephones, visitors, and instantaneous consumption keep work in the home in a state of constant motion and constant need of services. Under these conditions, a home employee can often feel non-productive.

Thus, when you consider the lack of end product in a home, the closeness and intimacy involved in home employment and a possible lack of managerial experience, promoting good work performance may take time, effort, and understanding.

Ten Steps Toward Effective Management

Begin to view yourself as a home executive and your home as a legitimate work place.

1. Establish fair pay and working conditions.

2. Define and redefine job expectations.

3. Review job performance every six months or so. Discuss with your employee whether or not you have met your mutual responsibilities. What problems are you and your employee having with the work or with each other? What solutions would be helpful? Encourage open communications. Job review time is a good time to grant a pay raise.

4. Offer on-the-spot, frequent praise. Sometimes it is helpful to recognize a job well done in the presence of others. Many appreciate public recognition.

5. Allow many opportunities for success. Give choices, incentives, bonuses, whatever it takes to help an employee feel valued and necessary, because they are.

6. Criticize rarely, on the spot, and in private. Criticize behavior, not the person. State the desired behavior you were looking for and how you may help achieve it. You may wish to stay close to the person and after the exchange has taken place, to touch them, smile, or put the complaint to rest.

7. Be flexible and sensitive to the needs of your employee.

8. Establish guidelines as to who is the manager and who is the employee. Try to keep this a simple one-to-one relationship. Your mother-in-law, girlfriends, really have no business managing the people who work in your home unless you have designated such a relationship.

9. Establish the management role of your spouse. In most homes, the husband plays a minor, supportive, and friendly role. If you and your husband direct an employee together, the employee may become confused and feel overpowered.

10. Do not overlook the possibility that you have hired a person who is not suited to perform the work they were hired to perform. Good managers know when to terminate employment.

Promoting Good Work Performance With an Employee Whose Good Work is Questionable

- Tell yourself that there are no bad employees, just poor managers. (Not always true — but a good starting point).
- Tell your employee of two months or five years that the work in your home is so important to you that you have purchased a book that will help you help them do their very best. You may have given some unclear directives or made some mistakes and you want to try to correct them right now.
- Please make sure that the salary is correct. Many times employeers were disatisfied with the work performance of an employee who was being underpaid.
- Re-read any section of this book that may have touched upon your area of disatisfaction — childcare, laundry, schedule, whatever.
- Re-read the ten steps of good management and try to communicate your needs. Use phrases such as "I feel angry, hurt, sad, etc., when you . . ."
- Listen to the responses of your employee.
- Set a time frame for the problems to be worked out.
- If you were unable to reach a compromise or satisfactory change in work performance, read step number ten and turn to the section on termination of employment.

Managing Two or More Workers

Effectively managing more than one household employee requires the following considerations:

- Make sure that you have provided enough room for each additional employee to live and work comfortably.
- Keep all salaries and working conditions as equitable as possible. Tell all employees not to compare wages and benefits with each other.

- Clearly define each employee's tasks and responsibilities. There may occasionally be some overlapping of duties, so encourage your employees to be flexible, understanding, and capable of sharing duties when necessary.
- Encourage all grievances such as job assignments or personal problems to be openly discussed. If, for instance, your long time cleaning person is offended because your new cook dictated some food or clean-up orders, or your childcare person complains about the laundry skills of your housekeeper, ask them to sit down with you and discuss their problems. Be a good listener and help your employees listen to the needs of others in your home. Help them work out reasonable solutions.
- Getting along with everyone in the household is a requirement for working in your home. Be prepared to let someone go who does not understand the importance of being compatable with others who work for you.
- If you employ one person who functions as a supervisor, you may wish to include this person in outlining other necessary job descriptions in your household and in interviewing potential assistants. A supervisor can usually be more effective if s/he has participated in a decision making process such as hiring.
- Large staffs require some accessibility to you. You may wish to set aside certain days and times to outline duties and to listen to employee job questions and personal concerns.
- Your responsibility is to provide a climate in which all employees can live and work successfully together. You and your family need to make sure each employee understands the uniqueness of his or her contribution to the household.

Ineffective Management Styles

In time, each employer develops her own style of management. You are really the last word on how to be an effective manager. Interviews and personal experience have uncovered home management styles which were not productive. These styles include:

The Tyrant

- No work is done to this employer's satisfaction.
- Information on how each task should have been performed is given after the job is completed.
- The Tyrant only finds fault. She ignores all good work which was accomplished.
- The Tyrant assumes no personal household responsibility. All housework is beneath her.
- The Tyrant is insensitive to employee needs.
- The Tyrant is a blamer; the lack of toilet paper in the bathroom, a broken fingernail, a child's bad school report, are somehow all the fault of the household employee.
- The Tyrant may or may not pay fairly. She usually employs others under the myth that servitude still exists in this country and is capable of demanding work well beyond the time limit and skill level for which she is paying.
- The Tyrant is so wrapped up in life's negatives that it would be difficult for her to find success and happiness anyway.

The Guilty Manager

- This employer usually feels guilty for having enough money to hire a household worker. Sometimes the guilty employer feels bad that people need jobs. Having a constant reminder of a system of economic differences right in her own home confuses this employer.
- Some Guilty Managers are not uncomfortable with economic differences but are uncomfortable with having someone else do housework because it makes them feel lazy. In fact, guilty people are often quite active.
- The Guilty Manager goes to extremes to pretend to herself and to her employee that this is not a "real job".
- The Guilty Manager is rarely involved in training or outlining job expectations for an employee. She thereby robs an employee of the ability to gain job satisfaction by performing assigned tasks.
- The Guilty Manager makes excuses as to why the employee does not perform in a certain manner. One employer cleaned her own stove because she felt that her employee had never seen a stove before and wouldn't know how to clean one.
- Guilty Managers usually do not have high job expectations. If the employee does not speak English, the guilty manager does not encourage her employee to learn this skill or other skill that could increase the employee's feeling of self worth.
- However, the Guilty Managers we interviewed usually had reasonably clean homes and moderately satisfied employees. Everybody just felt bad.

The Giver

- The Giver gives gifts, including old and new clothing. She often pays for personal services, such as beauty treatments. She gives willingly and often for two basic reasons. One, she wants her gifts to substitute for her inability to direct an employee — she hopes the employee will like her enough to do better work. The other reason the Giver may bestow presents on her employee is to take the place of paying minimum wage.
- The Giver usually remembers in great detail all gifts and favors she has granted to an employee and then feels hurt or angry when an employee does not perform favors for her.
- All gifts need to be given without strings. Working conditions need to be set out as such and not as favors.

The Missionary

- The Missionary believes she is taking in the problems of the world, giving the homeless a safe place to stay in exchange for "a little housework."
- A Missionary usually underpays. "What, give Esther a paid vacation? She likes it here. This isn't a factory job."
- While it is only human to treat employees with fairness and kindness, performing work in a home is work. Room and board, with or without kindness, is worth about $10 a day. Beyond that, employees need a salary.

The Hinter, Wisher, and Story Teller

- This employer avoids a direct confrontation with all employees. All work and needs are communicated through innuendo, hints, parables, or through the children. Sometimes employees respond in like manner so that the hints and signs become a game. Successful woman can communicate clearly. Ineffective managers keep wishing.

The Doormat

- The Doormat is often a mixture of the Guilty Manager, the Giver, and the Missionary. She abdicates her position of employer and gives this role to her employee. Thus, the Doormat devotes most of her days to working for her employee. She rearranges her home to suit her employee. She grants days off at any time her employee requests such. She pays for any services or product the employee claims to need. She becomes the furniture mover, the driver, the secretary, and anything else the people who work for her require.

The I Don't Care Manager

- The "I don't care what you do, just don't bother me with it" attitude does not help to keep employees satisfied with their work.
- Communicate what you do care about. Do encourage employees to seek answers to their own work problems, but you always need to assume the ultimate responsibility for what goes on in your home.

Be You

- There is some of every ineffective managerial style in each of us. Try to find the best, most effective style for you and your home by avoiding the common misconceptions and pitfalls of the sort listed above.
- Remember that laughter, warmth, and concern can help promote a good working relationship.

How Two Employers See Their Role as Home Managers

Sharon Brandon went from Doormat to effective home manager over a period of time. She discussed her role as follows:

Sharon Brandon:

> *"My role as an employer has evolved quite a bit. I wanted my earlier housekeepers to like me a lot. I wanted them to think that I was the cutest, nicest, most darling woman in town, and that working at our house was the most wonderful job there was. I used to scrub the house on Mondays so that Concha would return to an immaculate house on Tuesdays.*
>
> *My friends kept telling me that I was not in a popularity contest and that Concha would not disappear if I asked her to help me start dinner or to bring in the groceries. But I wouldn't believe them. I rarely asked Concha to do anything although she used to ask me for plenty. Silly me! I was so naive in those days. When I would leave to go marketing, she'd give me a list. She needed some stamps, she needed a bra, she had to send a money order. I was running errands for that woman and I never knew how to stop the situation. I was the same with the other live-ins we had in the first few years. If they had the nerve to ask, they got whatever they wanted from clothes to days off.*
>
> *With each succeeding housekeeper, my role has become clearer. I am not a bossy person, but I no longer pretend that I am not really the boss. My role is to be a good, kind, but assertive employer. I have gradually learned to take charge of things around here."*

June Stern:

> *"My role in relation to Marta was clearly defined before she moved in. I handed over to her total responsibility for the cleaning, laundry, and meal preparation. She is virtually self-employed in these areas; I am not her boss, nor do I want to be.*
>
> *We value and encourage her opinion. We give her plenty of praise, help her with any personal problems, and genuinely enjoy her as a person."*

CHAPTER FOURTEEN

Ironing Out the Wrinkles

Employing household help can always create rough spots and problems, especially when an employee lives in.

The previous chapters of this book have covered most areas of the work relationship that can cause difficulty, such as wages and working conditions, hiring, training, child care, and so forth. Any employment has employer/employee problems. Household employment is no exception. In fact, because a household employee may live in the employers' home, may be a woman alone in a foreign country, may be employed for the first time, may be without fellow workers, wrinkles can seem more substantial in a home employer/employee relationship.

Chapter Fourteen will present an overview of the most common areas of difficulty and will list suggestions on how to overcome these rough spots.

The Bottom Line

There are some forms of work in the house that are your responsibility and not the responsibility of an employee. All household workers interviewed expressed disgust at being asked to clean up dog droppings, cat boxes, animal cages, fish bowls, human excrement or vomit, and the like. There are some workers who may perform these chores voluntarily but, really, these bottom line duties are yours.

There are other forms of work that household employees dislike performing because performing these jobs either extend an eight hour day with no additional compensation, or are jobs more commonly performed by other classifications of household workers. Asking your daily cleaning person to wash the car, the dogs, or vacuum the pool can cause anger and resentment. Pay your children to wash the car or do yard work.

Try to avoid the Bottom Line.

Breaking or Damaging Personal Property

- Some damaged or broken household goods occur in every home no matter who works or lives there. When employing household help, be certain to explain this fact of life to your employee and then list the precautions you want followed to reduce the amount of property damage that could occur.
- Specify which items are never to be handled. Put away fragile or irreplaceable items; a cleaning person may have no idea whether a small glass held grape jelly or came over on the "Mayflower."
- Stress that all broken or damaged goods are to be reported immediately to you. If an object breaks, you want all the pieces collected and saved. If an appliance sounds strange or is not operating correctly, you need to know.

Stealing

- It is true that a household employee really has access to almost everything you own. It helps to have hired her through people you know and to have checked references very carefully.

- Stealing is not a common occurence. Most household workers need to be employed more than they need to sell a piece of your jewelry.
- Keep obvious temptation out of sight. Jewelry all over the house or lots of cash around gives the impression that you don't care enough about your money and possessions to put them away.
- If you do suspect stealing, check very carefully for evidence. You may call former employers and see whether they ever had similar suspicions. Try to remember who else had been in the house. Ask the employee to help you look for the missing items. Try not to lose a valued employee because of a false accusation.
- If your suspicions are correct, you can terminate the employment immediately. Or you and your employee can have a confrontation to determine whether it was more a case of stealing or of use without permission. Give the employee another chance if she was using the item without permission. But never keep a professional thief because you need someone to work in your house. Stealing was a rare complaint among our own experiences and the people we interviewed.

Gina — Live-in housekeeper:

"I hate it when they ask me where things are. I always think that the question means that I have taken things. It pains me when the mister asks if I have seen his tennis shorts. Like I would really wear them to the bus stop. From tennis shorts it always gets to ten dollar bills. I wish there was a way they could ask me to help find things without making it seem like I may have mailed all their right shoes to the one footed children of the world."

Avoid Scapegoating

Your personal problems and those of your employee can play a significant part in creating work problems between you. Many employers with their own sets of emotional, financial, and health difficulties can find their employees a ready, though not willing, targets for frustrations. Scapegoating an unhappy personal life on an employee is not fair. You can pay lots of people to help work out your personal life. Pay your household employee to maintain your home.

- When you know you have a lot of pressures or one week is going to be personally difficult for you, try warning your employee in advance.

Employee Personal Problems

The personal problems of employees were so much a part of difficult work situations that perhaps a brief overview of what these problems can be and what you could do to help would be beneficial.

In the days when the wealthy had servants, there was a saying about the personality of a household. "When the servants sing, so does the house." This is true today for any person who works in your home. If they are unhappy, their work and the mood of your home may reflect their unhappiness.

Financial problems — unpaid bills, debts, family needs, family emergencies:

- You may find this person extra work.
- Offer to pay an early Christmas bonus.
- Open a savings account in your name and theirs if this person is unable to open an account because they do not have a social security number. (You will receive an interest statement from the bank for taxation purposes, but the interest amount earned is rarely substantial).

- You may make a small loan. We advise against employee loans, especially for large amounts. If you must lend money, keep a repayment book and make out a repayment schedule that allows you to be repaid quickly.
- You may wish to go over monetary budget planning with your employee if she desires some help in this area.

Health Problems — health problems on the job are your problem too.

- You may take your employee to your doctor for immediate treatment or you may consult your doctor for clinic recommendations or to recheck a clinic's diagnosis or medication.
- You may wish to review any health care policy your employee carries or to investigate costs for enrolling your employee in a plan.
- Grant a sufficient amount of sick leave and set a monetary and sick leave limit to your involvement.
- The medications an employee may bring into your home are your business — check them by calling a doctor or pharmacist for an evaluation. We once found an employee using illegal mood elevators that were readily available in her country.

Pregnancy brings with it a set of age old problems for women.

- Try not to give too much advice, but do help your employee locate a woman's clinic where she can receive pregnancy counseling.
- If this employee lives in and wants to keep working, assist her in finding new day work and day care for the baby.
- Sometimes an employer will ask an employee to stay on with the baby, but such employment may not be in the best interest of the baby or the employee. Sometimes an employer does not want to find another worker and is making the offer to fulfill her own needs.

- **Personal relationship problems** — boyfriend and husband troubles — are often a source of unhappiness for any individual. You may wish to listen to these problems and offer help or counseling referrals if you think a counselor may be beneficial.

Consumer Problems:

- If an employee is troubled by a consumer problem, such as the purchase of defective merchandise, high interest loans, or the threat of utility shut off, you may offer to contact the agency, school, telephone company, etc., to assist your employee in resolving problems.
- You may help this person find competent legal help.

Extent of Employer Involvement

The extent of your involvement is up to you. Perhaps you may wish to set a time and monetary limit to the resolution of employee problems.

- An employee is an adult and needs the confidence, ability, and opportunity to work through her own problems.
- An employer is probably best off by being helpful and directional, but not completely taking over the handling of the personal problems of another.

The amount of involvement from the employers we interviewed ranged from absolutely none to quite extensive. One employer knew her worker and was upset by the immigration problems her family was having entering this country from Mexico. The employer drove to the border and smuggled the family in her own car. Interestingly, this employer said she was motivated more by the fear of losing the employee than by any real desire to help her.

Another woman sold her living room furniture and gave the money to a housekeeper who also wanted to bring her family here from a war-torn country. Her story follows.

Mary Beth:

> *"We were thrilled to be able to help her out and it's our feeling that, if the money never comes back, it's OK. It paid for three lives. They could be dead right now if it weren't for the money. It would be wonderful if we get repaid someday. We would take a vacation or furnish the living room, but it wouldn't mean anything to us, compared to the saving of lives. It's like the people during World War II who sent money to bring the Jews out of Germany, Austria, and Poland. I am sure that today they could not possibly remember what they would have bought with the money that they sent, but they certainly can tell you that money did buy life and freedom."*

Community Agencies

- Over the years, we have maintained a list of community agencies and referral services who have assisted various employees.
- You may wish to collect your own list of names and services such as clinics, legal aid societies, religious groups, consumer protection agencies, mental health clinics, children's health services, birth control information centers, discount pharmacies, and even private doctors, dentists, lawyers, accountants, and other professional people who will work with household employees for reasonable fees.

CHAPTER FIFTEEN

Parting of the Ways

The previous chapters have explained how to have a successful relationship with domestic employees. This chapter explains how the relationship may end.

"Can I Expect to Be Successful With My First Household Employee?"

- Perhaps. This book has attempted to give you every piece of information to make successful your first attempt in employing live-in help and live out help. Unfortunately, no book can give you or your first employee the extra ingredient that you both need, which is experience.
- Having several housekeepers, baby sitters, or drivers who only last a week or two is not uncommon. These terminations may be on their part or at your request. If you have three housekeepers or household employees during your first year of employing help, you may not really be failing, you may simply be gaining experience.

"When Do I Fire Someone Immediately?"

Immediate dismissal could result from any of the following situations:

- Child neglect. This covers irresponsible childcare, including leaving the children home alone, leaving with them in a car or other means of transportation without your permission, allowing or ignoring unsafe play, etc.

- Child abuse. This includes pinching, slapping, spanking, excessive teasing, harrassment, or sexual abuse.

- Failure to inform you of an accident, injury, illness, or of dangerous or forbidden behavior.

- Use of your car or other personal possessions without your permission.

- Expensive and excessive breakage.

- Willful destruction of property.

- Theft.

- Alcohol or drug abuse.

"How Do I Fire Someone on the Spot?"

- Tell the employee to pack or leave immediately. If this packing will take more than thirty minutes, tell s/he to pack as much as possible and you will deliver the rest. Call a cab if necessary and pay for it. Pay all wages owed immediately.

- To insure that no acts of revenge or anger occur, stay home until the employee is gone, even though you feel more comfortable leaving the house.

Inappropriate Employee Conduct

The following is a list of inappropriate employee conduct which usually does not result in immediate, on-the-spot firing, but should cause you to terminate the employment with notice. Consider this list carefully:

- She is less than a warm body when left in charge of the children. In addition to your two year old having never missed "The Johnny Carson Show" when you are out, his dress, food, and play indicate that your childcare person has no control so that your child's safety and health are in jeapordy.

- She demonstrates an unwillingness to work without constant supervision. Examples of this include having to be told to wash the breakfast dishes at dinner time, not returning clean clothes in the drawers for five days, vacuuming the living room at bedtime. We do not mean that she is unable to read your mind and unable to clean closet pulls or lamp shades on her own initiative.

- She exhibits severe and continued depression that is not caused by specific and/or temporary personal problems. Your employee seems sullen, angry, or tired.

- You are experiencing a build-up of minor annoyances but you cannot isolate anything major. Try to. The more specific you can be in describing the problems, the better chance you both have of working them out.

- She is critical of your life style or of you as a person. She may be jealous of your financial status or social life or family.

- She shows no consideration for your need for privacy. She is too free with advice or greets you with personal problems when you really need to be alone.

- She has a social life that disrupts your life. The phone never stops ringing, or girlfriends or boyfriends visit too frequently.
- You and she are involved in a power play or game of subversion so that things that you request are ignored. You must struggle to control your house and child. You question who is employer and who is employee.
- She exhibits an inability to get along with another member of your family. A clean house does not justify a personality conflict that hurts one of your children or your husband.
- She is not reliable. She does not show up for work and does not call in. She may be chronically late, leave early, take 4-6 hour rest periods, etc.
- Your employee repeatedly asks (directly or by innuendo) for gifts, time off, raises, used items. You are positive that you have been providing her with good working conditions, so the requests seem out of line.
- Your employee is a hypochondriac. You have had this person physically examined and are convinced that her health is good. You no longer care about the pain in her ear lobes.

"How Do I Know That My Problems With One Particular Person Are Serious Enough to Terminate Employment?"

- You are unhappy with the job performance 55% or more of the time.
- You have explained your unhappiness in specific behavioral terms and have outlined the behavioral changes you want her to make. You have explored and listened to her viewpoint and have suggested many compromises.

- You are certain that you are not unhappy in other areas of your life and are not really scapegoating your emotions onto her work performance.
- Believe us when we tell you that you can find someone who will work out better. Sometimes an employer keeps a person who only really meets 45% of their expectations because they do love this person as another member of the family. If you have reached this level of feeling, recognize it and resolve to become more content with your relationship.
- If you are becoming wrapped up in failures and resent spending a lot of energy on someone who is not your husband or child, you should ask her to leave. Your first priority is to yourself and to your family.
- A deteriorating situation usually gets worse. It is your right to fire a person whose work is not satisfactory. If you feel guilty, ease your guilt by helping her find another job, or by paying for job counseling. If you believe she could not work out suitably in any household, do not find her another job. Think of us.

"How Do I Terminate the Employment"

- If you and your employee are both honest people, you can tell her that her work is no longer necessary. Most jobs require that employers give a direct warning before they let someone go. You may give one warning also, but stick to it.
- Tell exactly when the last day will be. We prefer to make this last day soon.
- If being direct is not your style, you may tell her that you can no longer afford a live-in housekeeper. Then specify when her last day will be.

- Give her at least a week's severance pay, and pay all money earned up to her last day.

- You may wish to interview replacements *before* you ask your current employee to leave.

How To Handle Letting Someone Go Whom You Have Liked

- Sometimes your needs honestly have changed. You may be moving, experiencing financial reversals or upswings, or needing a different kind of household help, such as a day cleaner or workers who can cook and/or drive. Before you terminate a person who lacks skills you need, consider teaching the needed skills by hiring a teacher or by hiring additional people.

- If the person whom you are currently employing can no longer fulfill the employment needs of your home, you may explain to her that your needs have changed and she will no longer work for you.

- Give as much advance notice as you can, provide severance pay, and perhaps temporary work.

- Make every effort to find this employee another job. Write out a good reference; include your phone number, and give your employee copies.

What Are the Reasons That Employees Resign?

Again, this book has attempted to present the needs of your household employee. When you refuse to or are unable to meet her needs, she will leave.

The three most common reasons for leaving are money, money, and money. Other reasons include:

- **Obvious disparity** between her living conditions and the rest of the family's. For example, the food she eats is different from the rest of the family's or her bedroom is in shabby condition with less than the bare essentials.
- **Poor working conditions.** This could encompass no vacations or paid days off or raises, an abundance of work under constant demands, unruly and disrespectful children, too many animals, a work day that is longer than nine hours with no extra compensation, unkind criticism, anger, yelling, and a general feeling of no respect for work efforts and accomplishments.
- **Isolation.** There have been no means provided for socializing. There is little access to the phone, no visitors, no Saturday nights off, or the location of your home may be too far away from friends and family.
- **Change in her needs.** She may want to get married, get a different job, go to school, work days, return home, or have a baby.

What to Do When an Employee Gives Notice

- Talk with her. If the source of disastisfaction is something you are willing to negotiate, do so.
- More money is something you may *not* need to negotiate. If you have reread the salary scale presented in this book, and your pay falls within the correct amount, but your employee's financial needs exceed the standard, she may have no choice but to choose another location or a bigger house or different job whose longer hours will necessitate a salary increase.

- Try to anticipate a change in your workforce and plan accordingly. You can usually tell when an employee is going to leave before he or she gives notice. Pay attention to increased phone calls, circled "help wanted sections", and an increased number of complaints about the work.
- If you know that she is ready to move on, understand that employment in your home is really a dead end job. You cannot promote her to supervisor. Encourage her to seek personal and economic advancement. If she wants to leave to go to school, you may suggest a new schedule that will allow both employment in your home and the education she wants.
- If she wants to leave to get married or to have a baby, give her a party or shower.
- If you cannot meet her needs, for whatever reason, try to part amicably and stay in contact with her.

"Empty Closet" — When an Employee Leaves Without Notice

- Call her at her weekend home. You have her phone number and that of several of her friends so that you can locate her. If you must, have an interpretor close by for your phone call. Ask whether the problem can be discussed. If you believe that the problem is one that you can alleviate, offer to do so.
- She probably left without warning because she wanted to avoid a confrontation with you. By avoiding a confrontation, she believed that she was being respectful.
- If she is here illegally, she may be afraid that you will call immigration if she displeases or if you get angry at her. Although we have never known an employer to actually do this, the fear still exists.
- Begin to seek a new employee immediately.

Bigotry — For Losers Only

- A prejudiced employer causes a continued turnover of household employees. One family we interviewed has employed 38 live-in housekeepers over the last three years. They had a deep sense of bigotry against the ethnic group from which they were hiring employees. This prejudice kept causing workers to quit or to be fired for minor infractions.
- Racial prejudice can of course be the real reason an employer pays less, provides poor working conditions, complains about the quality of work performed, and so forth.
- The purpose of this book is not to do an employer/employee racial attitude study and its subsequent effect upon successful employment. The effects of such bigotry would be obvious.
- A book on household employment would be doing a disservice, however, if it did not touch on a more basic fact: many people lose good and valuable assistance in their homes because they believe that housework and the people who perform it are inferior.

Successful Relationships

The successful relationships we have seen and experienced are based upon a feeling of mutual interpersonal nourishment. Successful employers acknowledge their need for help and acknowledge and enjoy the affection they receive from employees. Likewise, many employees openly discuss and welcome the help and nurturing they receive from their employers. We all like to be needed. Some sense of dependency connects each one of us to another in a very real, human way.

How to have a successful relationship with the person who works in your home is really no secret. The employer and the employee need to satisfactorily meet the needs of one another. The services which are performed by a household worker must be paid for fairly. The person who performs these services must be granted human dignity. If the work to be performed is not communicated, prioritized, or considered valued, if the person who performs this work cannot meet his or her own needs, or is not treated with respect, or cannot respect the needs of the employer, there can be no relationship and no successful employment.

So now, *Get Ready* to use your most treasured commodity, time, wisely and to the fullest.

Get Ready to meet your goals in life.

Get Set to prepare your home as an efficient work place. Get set to enjoy your life and the lives of those you love.

Go — Get Help!

Emergency Information

With your help and guidance, most people working in your home can function in an emergency situation. There are extra worries for a mother leaving a child in the care of a non-English speaking employee, but all the suggestions below have been modified or expanded to include extra ideas or precautions for non-English speakers.

Getting Emergency Assistance

- Direct your employee on the first day to *always report any injury, accident, or illness to you*. This includes those injuries or problems that might seem minor or to have gotten better or which occurred to the employee. Chicken pox and impetago have been treated as diaper rash, and concussions ignored by employees who were not encouraged to report *everything*.
- Before the first day of employment, prepare an emergency telephone chart similar to the one on pages 176 and 177. Fill in the foreign language words if necessary. We wrote the Spanish as an example.
- Recheck the numbers on your list for accuracy. Do so every six months or so.

EMERGENCY TELEPHONE NUMBERS

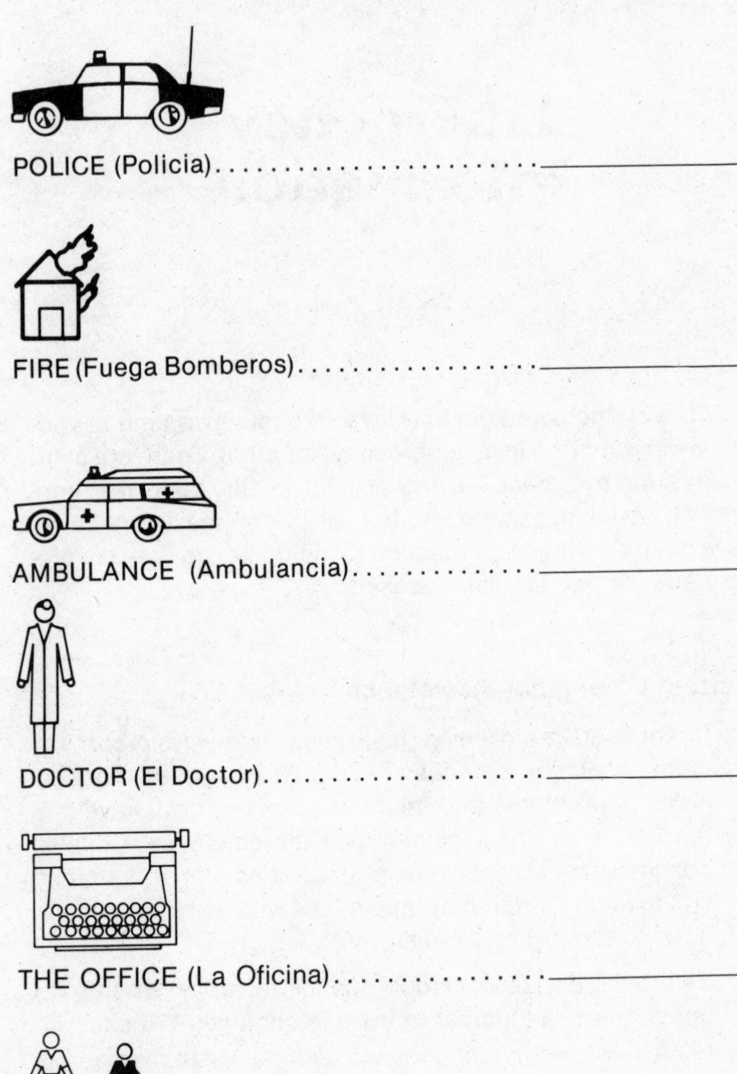

POLICE (Policia)........................ ______________

FIRE (Fuega Bomberos)................... ______________

AMBULANCE (Ambulancia).............. ______________

DOCTOR (El Doctor)...................... ______________

THE OFFICE (La Oficina)................ ______________

MY FRIENDS WHO HAVE HELP
(Mis Amigas Quien Tienen Empleada).... ______________

EMERGENCY TELEPHONE NUMBERS (Cont.)

MY FAMILY (Mi Familia)................ ______________

SECURITY GUARD (El Hombre de Guardia).. ______________

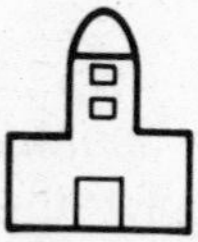

SCHOOL (La Escuela).................... ______________

INFORMATION LINE (Linea de Información) ______________

OTHER (Otros).......................... ______________

NAME AND ADDRESS OF THIS FAMILY
(Nombre y direccion de esta familia)

____

____

Tear out, write in foreign language words if necessary.
Please post.

- Many communities are now offering an emergency assistance and referral service for home emergencies. Locate this agency in your community and list their number. In many communities either this service or the police and fire, or both, provide foreign language emergency numbers.
- Make sure your employee knows someone who lives close by. Introduce your employee to other home employees in your neighborhood and/or other neighbors. There is a space for this neighbor's phone number on the telephone sheet. If your employee does not speak English, introduce her to someone who speaks her language and be certain their name and phone number appear on your list.
- Give copies of your emergency telephone list numbers to this neighbor and a secretary or relative who is usually home or near a phone. These people will then have the names of your doctors and other family members and friends if they need information to find you or to locate more help.
- Purchase a paging service if you are traveling enough hours a day to make it difficult to reach you. This service is often expensive but can allow your childcare person to beep or page you if there is an emergency.
- Teach your employee a series of calming phrases that could comfort your child until help arrives. Have her say, "I know it hurts," "Mommy will be here soon," "Try to let me hold you," and so forth.
- Prepare and sign a medical emergency treatment permission form to be used in case your child requires emergency treatment. Practice an emergency situation with your employee.

Prevention of Home Accidents

Re-evaluate your home in terms of preventing accidents.

- To prevent electrical fires or accidents, you may install plastic outlet covers. Explain their function to your housekeeper. Covers must be replaced on the outlet after it is used.
- Children should never be allowed to play with electrical appliances or outlets.
- No electrical appliances should be located near water. Avoid placing hair dryers in the sink or vacuuming a wet rug in the bathroom.
- Frayed cords or malfunctioning electrical equipment should be reported. An employee needs to understand overloaded circuits, to know where the circuit box is, and how to operate the circuit breakers if you aren't home.
- Label the circuit boxes accurately and show first aid advice for electrical shock.
- Always tell your housekeeper about people you expect to come to the door. For example, "I am expecting a delivery from a brown truck today," or "The plumber is coming in a white van." She is never to open the door for people whom she does not know or expect. Emphasize that this includes not opening the door for women or people who don't appear dangerous to her.
- If the person at the door says that they have an emergency and must use the phone, she is still not to let them in even if she understands the problem. She may make their call for them if you have told her that she may.
- The children should also not open the door for strangers or be allowed to talk to strangers when with her.
- All children's play must be supervised. Re-read "Activities Not Allowed" on page 128.

- All children's baths are supervised. Lower hot water temperature on your hot water heater to prevent accidental scalding.
- If there is a fire or an explosion in the home she should get the children and herself out of the home and run for help. She should be included in any evacuation drills that you do with the family.
- For earthquakes and natural disasters she should be shown a safe place to stay like a doorway or under a heavy table. She should know to avoid large areas of glass. If you need to, show her the gas turn off valve for your home. If you keep water, food, first aid, or other disaster supplies, show them to her. Again, include her in any drills or plans you and your family may have discussed.
- To prevent accidental poisoning, make sure to recap tightly all cleaning products and don't use any product whose contents are unfamiliar. All supplies are to be kept away from the children, out of their reach. The children are never to play in the medicine cabinet, in the garage, or where there are gardening supplies unless all dangerous substances are inaccessible. Review which of your plants are poisonous. If you have dangerous indoor or outdoor plants, keep them out of the reach of your children and point them out to your housekeeper. Check any plant that is brought into the house.
- Also check any medicines brought into your home as well as recommended dosages. Keep her room free of perfumes, cosmetics, and medications that the children could get into. Remember the first aid for poisons and to call for help.
- Post poison control phone numbers. Check with your poison control center to determine whether they provide information in foreign languages (usually they do not).
- No person may administer medication to your child without your permission.

First Aid

- Purchase a well illustrated first aid handbook such as *A Sigh of Relief* (Bantam Books) and go over this book with your childcare person. A well illustrated procedural book will help communicate procedures to a non-English speaker or non- reader. Check the front pages of your telephone directory for its first aid information.
- Many communities now offer telephone first aid information and a taped educational program available in several languages. Each emergency, such as bee stings or electrical shock, is given a separate code number. You may call one number, request information on each emergency, and listen to a tape explaining what to do. Check your central library or health agency.
- Rent or purchase a first aid video cassette and view it with your employee and your children. *Important*: The cassettes should not be used during an emergency situation. They are to provide general understanding *before* such an occurance happens.
- Prepare a first aid kit and explain all the items in it to your employee.
- Keep a poison chart and a first aid chart handy in your kitchen.
- You may wish to enroll your employee in a first aid course — especially if you are going to be away from home a lot.
- It is advisable that you go over this information as you ease your housekeeper into your employment. To present her with all the first aid information on her first day would be overwhelming. Be certain to check with your doctor for any of his recommendations or special precautions he recommends for your children.

Immigration Information

What to Tell Undocumented Employees

- All are entitled to a hearing before deportation.
- All may contact immigration attorneys for information concerning course of action and approximate cost of representation. Usually there is no charge for initial conversation, and there is no danger of deportation.

Expired Visas

- Visas may be renewable.
- Contact an immigration attorney.

When an Undocumented Worker is Detained by the Bureau of Immigration and Naturalization

- If an employee is picked up by immigration, they are entitled to a hearing provided they have *not* signed a voluntary deportation form. Advise an undocumented employee to sign *no* papers until an attorney so advises.

- Bond will be posted which may be paid through a bail bondsman or the employee (or the employer). We recommend an interest bearing form of payment.
- A hearing date will be established to determine the worker's right to remain in this country.
- Have this worker hire an immigration attorney immediately.

Applying for Legal Residency or the Green Card is Really White

- Contact and interview several immigration attorneys — check their bar standing with your local bar association. Inquire as to approximate time frame, charges, and predicted chances of this employee receiving legal status.
- The fee for obtaining legal residency status usually ranges from $1600 to $2200. Most employees pay this fee themselves in pre-arranged installment payments.
- You, as the employer, are asked to do three things:

  1. Fill out a statement of need proving that no one else could fill this job position. For instance, if your are employing a live-in person and travel often, or have health problems in your family that require late night or all night attendance — then you *need* a live-in employee.

  2. You must fill out a promise to employ form which states that you will employ this person when he or she receives their green card.

  3. You must run a three day classified advertisement offering your job to others hoping to prove that your employee is the only qualified applicant for the position.

- This entire process is currently taking two to three years.
- An employee with green card status is a legal resident. They may visit their native country and be joined here by spouse and/or children.
- There have been many undocumented household workers who immediately qualified for legal status but did not apply for it because they did not have accurate information about the legalization process.
- You, as an employer, will not be in legal difficulty for signing papers that essentially admit you have hired an undocumented worker. This lack of legal liability is based upon current law and could change.

Becoming a Citizen

- A person who has been a legal resident for five years, and is eighteen years old, is eligible for United States Citizenship.
- Many myths surround this process, such as the applicant is forced to insult his former country. These myths are not true.
- A naturalized citizen enjoys the full rights and privileges of all other citizens; they may return to their native country and they may bring in parents.
- Again, it is advisable that one contact an immigration attorney for complete details and costs.

INDEX

accidents 125, 127, 130, 175-181
accouterments 84-87
activities - children's 128-131
advertising 73
affording household help - Chapter Five
agencies 40, 48, 58, 74
aliens 33
animals 46, 157
answering your door 179
answering your phone 89
appearance 77, 93
appliances 96, 104, 123, 130
arguments 30
attic 101
attorney, immigration — see Appendix
au pair 40, 93
automobile 39, 93, 114
automobile insurance 114

B

babies — Chapter Eleven
babysitters 100 — Chapters 10, 11, 12
basement 101
baths — children 99, 179
baths — employee 93
bathroom 100
bed making 88, 104
bedroom 84
beginning employment — Chapter 8
beginning level 51
behavior problems 136
benefits 53-59
biannual cleaning jobs 101
birthday — as day off 53
birthday — gifts 93
boyfriends 92, 162
breakfast 98
breakage 158
budget — Chapter Five, 161
Bureau of Immigration and Naturalization — see Appendix
Bureau of Internal Revenue 55
burns 179-180
buses 87
butler 28, 29

C

cars — see automobile
chauffeur see driver
checks 58
check-up 88
chest X-ray 88
childcare — Chapters 10-12
children — Chapters 10-12
citizen 182-184
cleaning person 38, Chapters Four-Nine
cleaning supplies 97, 98
cleaning training — Chapter Nine
classes — childcare 131
classes — English 91
classified 73
clinics 161
clothes 87, 93, 127
companion 41, 113
communication 149
community agencies 163
consultants 115
consumer information 162
convalescent home 113
convalescent patient 44
cook 39
cooking 110
cosmetics 180
costs — Chapters Three-Five, Chapter Seven

D

daily cleaning jobs 98-100
damage 158
dangers 130, 131, 179, 180
dating 92
day classes 91
day cleaner 38, Chapters Four-Nine
days off 53
deliveries 179
deodorant 85
deportation 182
diets 85, 113
dinner 85, 88, 111
dinner parties 44
dinners out 87
discipline 136, 137
dish washers 96, 99
dishes 62
doctor 88, 161, 181
dogs 113, 157, 158
drivers 39, 114, 115
drying 106
dusting 95, 100

E

earthquake 180
education 80, 91
elderly 41
electricity 104
emergency 32, 175-180
Employer Identification Number 55
employment agencies —
see Agencies
employment taxes 54-47
England 40
English 29, 31, 51, 91
entertaining 44, 54
equipment 96-98, 104, 158
errand person 41
experience levels 51
expired visas 182
exploitation 34
extra pay 54
eyesight 88

F

financial considerations —
Chapter Five
fire(to) 166-168
fires 179, 180
first aid 181
food for employees 86
food storage 106
friends 90-91

G

gifts 93
governess 40, 119
green card 183
groceries 108
grocery shopping 109
grooming 93
guests — employee 90, 91
guests — employer 44, 54
guilt 27, 152

H

handicapped 41
harassment 166
health check 88
health care 57
heavy work 42
hiring — Chapter Six
holiday — pay 54
home remodeling 54
hours of work — Chapter 3, 98-100
housekeeper defined 42
houseman 42

illegal 33, 182
illness 161, 166
immigration 182
improper feeding 135
inappropriate conduct 167
income tax 55
inexperienced 51
ineffective management style 151-154
infants — Chapter Eleven
injuries 175
insurance 57
instruction — see Training
intermediate level 51
Internal Revenue 55
interview 75-77
introducing an employee to your home — Chapter Seven
introductions 84
involvement — with personal problems 162
ironing 107

J

jealousy 133
jewelry 158, 159
junk 95, 127

K

keys 93

L

lateness 168
laundry help 39, 100
laundry instruction 106
laundry sorting 106
laundry supplies 106
legal — advice 182
legal — residency 183
levels of experience 51
lists 117, 177
literacy 80
live-in housekeeper — see Housekeepers
live-out housekeeper — see Housekeepers
living room — employee 84-87
living room — employer 100
lodging 49, 50, 84
long distance phone calls 88, 89

M

maid 28
mail 104
market — see grocery store
management — Chapter Thirteen
maximum work day 49, 50
meals — employees 85
meals — for children 110, 111
meals — for family 110
meal service 112
medicine 180
minimum wage 49
missed work days 53
missing items 158
mother-in-law 148
moving 44

N

nanny 40, Chapters 10-12
newspaper 73
night school 91
night socializing 92
notice 167-169
nursing home 41
nutrition 102, 110, 111

O

older people 41
overnight guests 44, 90
overtime 49-50, 54

P

paid days off 54
papers — important 104
papers — legal 104
papers — personal 104
part-time help 43, 44, 62
parties 54
pay period 58
payroll deductions 54-57
payroll taxes 55, 56
personal problems —
Chapter Fourteen
pets 113, 157
phone — see Telephone
plane fare 40
plants care 100, 115
plants — dangerous 180
poisoning 180, 181
power play 168
privacy 30, 31, 168
professional cleaning supplies 97
professional employment level 51
prohibited activities —
children's 130
public transportation 87

Q

quitting — Chapter Fifteen

R

radio 85
raises 58
recreation 127-130
references 74, 78
rent-a-wife 29, 41
residency 182-184
retirement plan 57
room 30
room and board 49, 50
rules — Chapter Seven

S

safety 127, 175, 180
salary levels 51
sale — house 44
sample schedule 98-100
saving accounts 160
scapegoating 160
schedule 98
seamstress 39
security system 84, 177
servant 28
serving 112
sewing 39
shoes 93
shopping 41
sick — children 20, 180
sick — employees 57, 161
sick days 52
skill level 51, Chapter Nine, 170
snacks 126
smoking 76
smoke detector 84
soap 85
socializing 90, 168
social life 90-92
social security 58
staffs 149, 150
stains 107
starting
employment — Chapter Seven
salary 48, 51
time 98-100
stealing 158, 159
storing food 106
strangers 179
supplies — cleaning 97-99

T

table — clearing 112
table — setting 99, 102, 112
tape recorder 116, 130
taped information 116, 181
tax
  credit 66
  information 54-57
  withholding 56
taxi cabs 166
teachers 115
teaching — Chapter Nine
telephone
  answering 89
  for employees 88
  emergency use 175-178
television 85
temporary 43, 44, 80
termination — Chapter Fifteen, 141
theft 158, 159
toys 127-130
training — Chapters Nine and Eleven
trains 87
tuberculosis 88
two or more employees 37, 149, 150

U

unemployment insurance 56
uniforms 87
unpaid days off 53

V

vacations — employee 53
vacations — employer 144, 145
vacuum cleaners 104
valuables 158, 158
video cassettes 131, 180
visas 182-184
vision test 88
visiting friends 90-92

W

wages — Chapters Three, Four and Five
washing machine 106, 107
washing products 106, 126
weather changes
  household responsibilities 105
  children's clothes 127
window washing 101
withholding tax 54-56
working conditions — Chapter Seven
workman's compensation 56
work permit 183

XYZ

X-ray 88
yearly cleaning schedules 101
yearly pay evaluations 58, 148

SELECTED BIBLIOGRAPHY

Green, Martin I, *A Sigh of Relief.* New York: Bantam Books, 1976. A well illustrated (for the non-English reader) book on first aid procedures and safety practices.

Moore, Alma C. *How to Clean Everything.* New York: Simon & Schuster, 1971.

Aslett, Don. *Is There Life After Housework?* Cincinnati: Writer's Digest Books, 1981. Professional cleaning advice about simplifying and organizing household cleaning jobs which can be taught to cleaning help.

Blanchard, Kenneth and Johnson, Spencer. *The One Minute Manager.* New York: William Morrow and Company, Inc., 1982. Teaches one how to be an efficient and effective manager of people.

Young, Pam & Jones, Peggy. *Sidetracked Home Executives.* New York: Warner Books, 1981. Again many organizational ideas are helpful teaching to home employees.

Spock, Benjamin. *Baby and Child Care.* New rev. ed., New York: Pocket Books, 1976.

Stein, Sara Bonnett. *The Kids' Kitchen Takeover.* New York: Workman Publishing Company, 1975. Many easy to do kitchen activities for childcare person and your child to enjoy.

Sunset Books & Sunset Magazine, eds. *Easy Basics for Good Cooking.* Menlo Park: Lane Publishing Company, 1982. Well illustrated, up-to-date, basic cooking principles and recipes; good book for teaching someone how to cook.